D1577943

"Vatican II's declaration *Dei Verbum* has proven to [be one of the] important and lasting actions of the Council, injecting new life and vigor into the biblical renewal of the Catholic Church. Ronald Witherup, SS, is, as he notes, a 'product' of this renewal—becoming a noted Catholic voice in the interpretation of the Scriptures. His dedication and skill are on display here as he provides an in-depth but very accessible commentary on the Council's statement and lays out its meaning for the life of the Church today."

>—Donald Senior, CP
>President Emeritus and Professor of New Testament
>Catholic Theological Union

"Vatican Council II's *Dogmatic Constitution on Divine Revelation* was a life-changer for the twentieth-century church. In this splendid little volume, *The Word of God at Vatican II: Exploring Dei Verbum*, Fr. Ron Witherup tells us how it came about, what it said, and some of what happened as a result. It's a must-read for every religious educator in the English-speaking world."

>—Raymond F. Collins
>Department of Religious Studies
>Brown University

"Ron Witherup's book on *Dei Verbum*, Vatican II's dogmatic constitution on divine revelation, is a gem. He provides, in effect, a clear and accessible 'exegesis' of a document whose import and impact continue fifty years later. In addition, Fr. Witherup sets *Dei Verbum* in its historical context and offers practical suggestions for its ongoing appropriation. I highly recommend this book, especially for Bible study groups and parish education classes."

>—Thomas D. Stegman, SJ
>Associate Professor of New Testament
>Boston College School of Theology & Ministry

"In order to deepen both our relationship to Scripture, and to God, we must understand what we read and pray with. As a writer and speaker, I often refer to *Dei Verbum*, frequently urging others to study this essential document as a way of deepening their understanding of Sacred Scripture. In this treasure of a book, Ronald Witherup, SS, offers those who are familiar with *Dei Verbum*, as well as those who are just beginning, new and important insights into the Word of God."

>—Fran Rossi Szpylczyn
>Catholic writer and lay minister
>Albany, New York

"Ronald Witherup's treatment of the great Constitution on Divine Revelation provides the reader with an excellent tour of one of the most important church documents of the last five hundred years. It's both scholarly and yet very accessible. For teachers, preachers, and pastoral ministers, this book is essential reading because it embraces so fully the central role of the inspired Word of God in the life of today's Church."

— Bill Huebsch
Author of *The Spiritual Wisdom of Saint John XXIII*

"A book for all seasons—but especially today! As our commitment to hearing and living the Word of God deepens and as we continue to comprehend the treasure, ramifications, and challenges of the Second Vatican Council, Fr. Witherup takes us on a journey of understanding and appreciation of Scripture and one of the Council's foundational documents, the Dogmatic Constitution on Divine Revelation, a journey that is unequalled. A survey of the history, the meaning, and implications of *Dei Verbum*, as well as practical suggestions for the future, are succinctly summarized with comprehensive clarity and fervent fidelity. This book is ideal for individual and group reflection and study, and then needs to be kept on a near-by bookshelf for continual reference."

— Janet Schaeffler, OP
Author, Retreat and Adult Faith Formation Facilitator

The Word of God at Vatican II

Exploring *Dei Verbum*

Ronald D. Witherup, SS

LITURGICAL PRESS
Collegeville, Minnesota

www.litpress.org

Nihil Obstat: Reverend Robert Harren, *Censor deputatus.*

Imprimatur: ✠ Most Reverend Donald J. Kettler, J.C.L., Bishop of Saint Cloud, Minnesota. February 14, 2014.

Cover design by Ann Blattner. Photo courtesy of Thinkstock by Getty Images.

2	3	4	5	6	7	8	9

Library of Congress Cataloging-in-Publication Data

Witherup, Ronald D., 1950–
    The word of God at Vatican II : exploring Dei verbum / Ronald D. Witherup, S.S.
        pages   cm
    ISBN 978-0-8146-3556-8 — ISBN 978-0-8146-3581-0 (ebook)
    1. Vatican Council (2nd : 1962–1965 : Basilica di San Pietro in Vaticano). Constitutio dogmatica de divina revelatione.   2. Revelation—Catholic Church.   3. Bible—Study and teaching—Catholic Church.   I. Title.
    BX8301962.A45 C79   2014
    231.7'4—dc23   2014001605

In Memory of
Saint John XXIII
(b. 1881; pope, 1958–1963)

Contents

Acknowledgments

This book came into being at the invitation of Little Rock Scripture Study, with whom I have had the privilege of working for many years on various projects, most recently, the *Little Rock Catholic Study Bible*.

I congratulate Little Rock Scripture Study (LRSS) on its fortieth anniversary (2014) and express my sincere gratitude for all they have done to foster an authentic ministry of the Word in the Diocese of Little Rock and far beyond. They have admirably fulfilled the vision of *Dei Verbum* (DV) that called for the broad dissemination of the word of God through excellent resources (DV 25). I have always respected their professionalism and their dedication to promoting the word of God. I sincerely thank the director of LRSS, Catherine "Cackie" Upchurch, who read through the manuscript with a helpful eye and also provided a separate booklet of study questions for those who want to explore the topic in more depth. I thank also the rest of the staff of LRSS: Lilly Hess, Cliff Yeary, Sister Susan McCarthy, RDC, and Nancy Lee Walters. Along with Cackie, they make a wonderful team! I am also grateful to Bishop Anthony B. Taylor of Little Rock, and his farsighted predecessors, for recognizing the value of this important ministry in his diocese and for supporting its dissemination far and wide.

As the reader will note, I dedicate this book to the memory of Saint John XXIII, "Good Pope John" as he was often called. He courageously oriented the church toward the third Christian millennium by convoking the Second Vatican Council (1962–65), the golden anniversary of which we are celebrating (2012–15). His bold pastoral vision of a "new Pentecost" for the church, rooted in the Sacred Scriptures, also helped give direction to the document explored in this book. In fact, as will be recounted later in chapter 1, one can say he almost "conceived" the constitution by one bold action.

I add two practical comments about this book. Although there are no footnotes in it, the text of *Dei Verbum* does have forty-one footnotes, which are included with the text of the constitution. These have been assembled as endnotes at the end of chapter 2 and may be consulted as needed. I have also included a glossary of important terms at the end of the book. The first occurrence of these words in the text is marked with an asterisk (*).

Finally, I must express some words of appreciation to those who helped with the final production of this book. I am enormously grateful to the entire staff at Liturgical Press for their constant support and expert guidance, especially Peter Dwyer, Barry Hudock, Andy Edwards, Colleen Stiller, Stephanie Nix, Stephanie Lancour, and Michelle Verkuilen. Also deserving my gratitude for numerous favors and for his friendship over the years is Father John R. Donahue, SJ, who graciously read the manuscript with care, gave me many helpful pointers, and saved me from a few gaffes. I alone, however, am responsible for any shortcomings.

May the word of God flourish and help bring peace to the earth!

R.D.W.
Memorial of Saint Jerome, 2013

CHAPTER ONE

A Brief History of *Dei Verbum*

If, as the saying goes, "a picture is worth a thousand words," then an image from the Second Vatican Council (1962–65) may provide an inspiring starting point for this book. Each of the four sessions of the council saw the procession and enthronement of a fifteenth-century book of the gospels in the midst of the council fathers when they met in plenary session, in accordance with an ancient practice from the fifth century AD. When Pope Paul VI attended such sessions, he carried the ornate book himself. There is no more powerful symbol of the centrality of the word of God in the life of church. In the very presence of the sacred word of God—representing the living Word himself, Jesus Christ—the council fathers undertook the arduous task of an ecumenical* council to confront the needs of the modern world. The inspired word of God would rekindle the spark of the Catholic faith in the mid-twentieth century. The harbinger of this new hope founded on Sacred Scripture was a rather short document, a dogmatic* constitution on the concept of divine revelation, which was one of the last documents to be approved by the council but which would breathe new life into the role the Scriptures would play in the Catholic Church for generations to come.

Dei Verbum, the Dogmatic Constitution on Divine Revelation, is without doubt one of the most important teachings to come out of Vatican Council II. It is one of four "constitutions"—and only two *dogmatic* constitutions—the ecumenical council issued. It consequently holds the highest level teaching authority (magisterium*) in the church. The document also has one of the most interesting origins among the documents of the council. Before addressing this history, though, a word about the text itself is essential.

The Text of *Dei Verbum*

There is no final, definitive text of *Dei Verbum* in English. The official text is in Latin, as is the case with all the documents of the council. Some church authorities have called for a definitive translation into various modern languages, but that would pose a challenge. Let me use the analogy of the Bible to explain why. Just as the Bible needs to be studied in the original languages (Hebrew, Aramaic, Greek) with modern translations updated from time to time, so such crucial ecclesial documents as these, which come from an ecumenical council, can benefit from periodic retranslation. As time moves on, comprehension of such important texts that touch the identity of the church can change and be profoundly deepened. Professional commentaries exist that recount almost word for word the formation of *Dei Verbum*. These resources help us to understand the constitution in its original context as it was being framed. Revisiting this analysis from time to time can only be, in my judgment, beneficial. So insisting on a *definitive* modern translation would likely be ineffective, since the original must be consulted anyway.

Be that as it may, dealing with the Latin original cannot totally be avoided. Thus, I will occasionally point out specific Latin terms that help us understand the profound teaching of this document. We might remember that not only were the documents of Vatican II written in Latin but virtually all the presentations given during the council were also delivered in Latin, a language many bishops could barely understand as an oral or conversational language. (Needless to say, Latin experts had a lot of work behind the scenes functioning as translators!) One exception was Maximos IV Sayegh (1878–1967), the patriarch of the Greek Melkite Church, who insisted on addressing the council in French, and who made several highly influential interventions during the council. His reason is interesting. He maintained that Latin was not the language of the *universal* church but of the Roman church of the West, the Latin Rite. Other Catholic rites use diverse languages in their rituals, such as Greek, Syriac, Coptic, and Armenian, among others. In any case, the final text of *Dei Verbum* is in Latin and must be understood from this perspective. In this book, we will keep such references to a minimum in contexts where the proper sense of *Dei Verbum* seems to require an understanding of the Latin text. Also, whenever necessary, the reader can consult the glossary in the back of the book to refresh one's memory of unfamiliar terminology.

As regards English translations that are available, no one text can be said to be the best. Several good ones are recommended, as mentioned in the "Further Reading" section at the conclusion of this book. The Vatican website (www.vatican.va) also offers a useful one that is easily available. For convenience, this book uses the Austin Flannery edition, which has been inserted into the text by numbered paragraphs. Unless otherwise noted, it is the translation cited. With the publisher's permission, I have made only minor corrections to this text, mainly corrections of typos or evident grammatical errors. Now to a synopsis of the history.

Concise History of *Dei Verbum*

Originally titled "A Schema* of a Dogmatic Constitution on the Sources of Divine Revelation," the first draft of the document offered to the council fathers (that is, the bishops) during the first session of the council in the fall of 1962 was drafted by a preparatory theological commission dominated by officials from Roman congregations or dicasteries* (the Curia*). This draft consisted of five chapters, outlined in the chart below.

Schema of first draft, On the Sources of Revelation (Latin, *De Fontibus Revelationis*)	
Chap. 1	The Double Sources of Revelation
Chap. 2	The Inspiration, Inerrancy, and Literary Form of Scripture
Chap. 3	The Old Testament
Chap. 4	The New Testament
Chap. 5	Holy Scripture in the Church

The drafters assumed that the council fathers would simply adopt such a document, perhaps with minor modifications or suggestions for improvements. To everyone's surprise, numerous council fathers, including the elderly and widely respected cardinal Archbishop Achille Liénart from Lille (France), spoke strongly against the draft. They boldly called for it to be taken off the table and to be entirely reworked. They viewed both the tone and content of the document as problematic. A young theologian by the name of Joseph Ratzinger, later Pope Benedict XVI, who served as an expert advisor (Latin, *peritus**) at the council was one who privately expressed the discontent. He pointed out the excessively negative and defensive tone of the document and its lack of theological finesse.

I must note here that more recent scholarship on *Dei Verbum* has shown that the initial negative reaction of some council fathers to the first draft (technically called a "schema") of the constitution may have been due in part to a prejudgment and an exaggerated fear of the influence of the Roman officials who had formulated it. An examination of *De Fontibus Revelationis* has shown that it was perhaps a bit more nuanced than was recognized. Nevertheless, the fact remains that many council fathers strongly opposed the first schema and wanted it entirely redrafted.

As a result, there was no way the draft could get the required two-thirds vote to pass. Neither could the opponents muster a two-thirds majority to remove it for redrafting. For a week it looked as if the council would hit a major roadblock in its infant stages. Then the next day, unexpectedly, Pope John XXIII himself intervened, something he was most reluctant to do and, in fact, rarely did during the council. The pope announced that the draft would indeed be sent back for major reworking. To this end, he appointed two cardinals, who happened to be on opposite theological poles regarding the document, to lead a special "mixed" commission to hammer out an entirely new text to bring back to the council fathers. One was Italian Cardinal Alfredo Ottaviani (1890–1979), head of the Holy Office (now the Congregation for the Doctrine of the Faith) and also head of the Doctrinal Commission that had drafted the first schema. The other was German Cardinal Augustin Bea (1881–1968), head of the Secretariat for Promoting Christian Unity (now the Pontifical Council for Christian Unity) and a biblical scholar. The opposing forces could scarcely have been better represented. Yet both had to work together, along with some other council fathers and experts, to come up with a new, more acceptable draft constitution. In this sense, one can say John XXIII almost "created" this document by his bold action.

The entire process of drafting a new dogmatic constitution on revelation would be very complicated and not be completed until the last session of the council in the fall of 1965. The constitution went through various other drafts and was subjected to many amendments over the next three years before it would finally be approved by a resounding affirmative vote on November 18, 1965, scarcely before the council itself ended on December 8, 1965. All parties recognized that the final dogmatic constitution was in many ways a compromise document. It shows a lot of give-and-take, which means that one can sometimes find justification in it for positions that are at least in tension, if not outrightly opposed to one another. That being said, *Dei Verbum* is nonetheless a *dogmatic* constitution adopted by an ecumenical council and promulgated by Pope Paul VI. It thus constitutes the church's highest teaching authority on the theme of divine revelation. Moreover, its less doctrinal focus and more pastoral tone more closely matched the design of the council as expressed by John XXIII, who had convened the council. It also influenced every subsequent church teaching on Scripture to the present, an issue we will examine more closely in chapter 3.

Comparing the outline of the final dogmatic constitution (with paragraph numbers in parentheses) and the first edition, as placed side by side in the chart below, helps to clarify what some of the problems with the earlier draft were.

A Comparison of the First and Final Drafts

Schema of first draft *De Fontibus Revelationis*		Schema of final document *Dei Verbum*	
(On the Sources of Revelation)		**(The Word of God)**	
		Prologue (1)	
Chap. 1	The Double Sources of Revelation	Chap. 1	Divine Revelation Itself (2–6)
Chap. 2	The Inspiration, Inerrancy, and Literary Form of Scripture	Chap. 2	Transmission of Divine Revelation (7–10)
		Chap. 3	Sacred Scripture: Its Divine Inspiration and Interpretation (11–13)
Chap. 3	The Old Testament	Chap. 4	The Old Testament (14–16)
Chap. 4	The New Testament	Chap. 5	The New Testament (17–20)
Chap. 5	Holy Scripture in the Church	Chap. 6	Sacred Scripture in the Life of the Church (21–26)

Four differences are quite telling. First, the final title does not mention "sources" for divine revelation, which had clearly implied that Scripture and tradition* were two separate sources. In fact, the constitution would ultimately speak only of one source of God's self-revelation that had two aspects, Scripture and tradition, viewed as intimately interrelated.

A second observation is that the final version begins in a much more personal way. The addition of an introductory prologue, with a biblical citation from the First Letter of John, orients the constitution in a highly personalistic direction. Some interpreters see in this prologue an orientation for the entire council, even though *Dei Verbum* was one of the last documents to be adopted. It speaks about divine revelation itself in terms of God's outreach to humanity, an act of divine communication. It does not begin with a discussion of sources leading into a presentation of technical questions right away. This personal approach would also orient future discussions of revelation and Scripture for many decades to our own day.

Third, we note that *Dei Verbum* contains no mention in the chapter headings of "inerrancy,"* though the topic is discussed in chapter 3 of the constitution. The earlier draft had essentially jumped quickly to the notions of inspiration,* inerrancy, and literary form to bolster the truth of Scripture narrowly understood, whereas *Dei Verbum* would nuance these ideas considerably. It avoided altogether the word "inerrancy" in favor of a more refined discussion of how the Holy Spirit preserves the message of Scripture from error.

Finally, with the addition of a prologue and a more subtle presentation of the last three chapters on the Old Testament, the New Testament, and the role of Scripture in the church's life, *Dei Verbum* emphasized its pastoral focus, a hallmark of the council. From the beginning of the council, with John XXIII's opening address titled *Gaudet Mater Ecclesia* (Mother Church Rejoices), the goal of orienting the church's conciliar teaching in a pastoral way was evident. *Dei Verbum* embodies this pastoral approach. ("Pastoral" here does not mean lightweight, insignificant, or without doctrinal content; it refers to the pope's goal of reaching out to the modern world to help the faith to be understood better.)

What does this history tell us? It bears testimony to the complex process of ecumenical councils, of which there have only been twenty-one in the history of the church, starting with the First Council of Nicaea (AD 325). (In this context "ecumenical," from Greek *oikoumenē*, means universal rather than interdenominational.) It also demonstrates both the continuity and distinctiveness of Vatican II in relation to other councils. *Dei Verbum* issues no condemnations (the technical word "anathema"*) of errors or critiques of other Christian denominations, nor does it proclaim any new dogmas. It calmly, directly, clearly, and pastorally presents a Catholic understanding of the mystery of God's self-revelation to humanity. In doing so, the council fathers desired to invite all the people of God to eat and drink of the one table of divine nourishment, understood as Scripture and tradition in their deepest meaning. The lack of a defensive and aggressive tone helps make the constitution more inviting. While *Dei Verbum* clearly stands in continuity with prior church teaching on the topic of revelation, notably the Council of Trent (1546–63) and Vatican Council I (1869–70), it nonetheless charted a new course to steer the church into the challenging waters of modern life.

Influence of Church Documents on *Dei Verbum*

Virtually all church documents have been influenced in one way or another by previous church teachings. *Dei Verbum* is no exception. The following chart gives a thumbnail sketch of the influence of certain key church documents on the final edition of *Dei Verbum* adopted at Vatican II on November 18, 1965, the anniversary of the publication of Pope Leo XIII's encyclical* letter *Providentissimus Deus* in 1893. A short narrative explanation follows.

Major Documents Influencing *Dei Verbum*

Document Title	Author	Date	Content	Influence on *Dei Verbum*
Decretum Primum On the Canonical Books *Decretum Secundum* On the Latin Vulgate	Council of Trent, fourth session	1546	Called for respect of both Scripture and the apostolic traditions of the church; established the limits of the Catholic canon* of Scripture, both the Old and New Testaments,	DV 7, 9, 11

Table continued on pages 8–9

Document Title	Author	Date	Content	Influence on *Dei Verbum*
			and gave precedence to Saint Jerome's Latin Vulgate* translation from the original languages	
Dei Filius Dogmatic Constitution on the Catholic Faith	Vatican Council I	1870	Defined the Scriptures as sacred literature inspired by the Holy Spirit, with God as their "author"	DV 6, 7, 8, 10, 11, 12
Providentissimus Deus Encyclical letter on Scripture study	Pope Leo XIII	1893	Cautiously promoted modern scientific study of Scripture while affirming the basic historicity of the biblical books	DV 11, 24
Divino Afflante Spiritu Encyclical letter on promoting biblical studies	Pope Pius XII	1943	Encouraged Catholic scholars to use modern historical critical methods* of Bible research and to pay attention to the original languages and literary forms in the Bible; usually considered the Magna Charta of modern Catholic biblical study	DV 11, 23

Sancta Mater Ecclesia Instruction on the Historical Truth of the Gospels	Pontifical Biblical Commission	1964	Describes the gospel traditions as consisting of three levels: (1) historical life of Jesus (2) preaching of his first followers (3) the writings of the evangelists	DV 19 adopts some of the language and the threefold schema of the gospel traditions, while affirming the basic historicity of the gospels

The Council of Trent (1546–63)

For modern Catholicism the Council of Trent looms large as a significant influence on the life of the church. It was the first council following the Protestant Reformation, and it initiated the Catholic reform that came to be known as the Counter-Reformation. In designing *Dei Verbum* the council fathers drew explicit attention to this council, along with Vatican I, to underline the continuity in Catholic teaching on revelation. But two observations help to keep this fact in perspective.

First, the teaching at Trent is relatively brief and in fact does not discuss revelation itself. Rather, that council finally settled the question of the extent of the "canon"* (from Greek *kanōn*, "norm") of the Scriptures. For Catholics, the Old Testament consists of forty-six books, and the New Testament of twenty-seven books, for a total of seventy-three books of Sacred Scripture. (Protestants and Orthodox have a somewhat different list of canonical books.) Trent also underlined that God is the real "author" of the biblical books, and that the church has the definitive authority and obligation to oversee authentic interpretation of the Bible. It also gave priority to the Latin Vulgate edition of the Bible over the original languages.

Second, at the time of Vatican II scholarship on the Council of Trent had matured significantly. Previous narrow interpretations of Trent were shown to be exaggerated. Although the decrees at Trent conclude with anathemas, condemnations of those who would go contrary to the church's teaching, modern scholarship showed that Trent was less rigid and more nuanced than had usually been presumed. On the question of the "sources" of revelation, for instance, Trent never actually taught that there were two of them. It simply said that Scripture (both Old and New Testaments) and the oral or written traditions of the church on faith and morals should be recognized "with equal measure of piety and reverence" (Latin, *pari pietatis affectu ac reverentia* [First Decree, April 8, 1546]). Most important, however, is to recognize that Trent, in comparison to Vatican II, focused on the more "propositional" aspects of revelation rather than the personal. Uppermost at Trent was the content of the faith, rather than its relational aspects. *Dei Verbum* affirms these teachings, but then proceeds to nuance them with the personal, dynamic, and dialogical concepts that marked the final dogmatic constitution.

Vatican Council I (1869–70)

As the council closest to Vatican II (although almost one hundred years earlier!), one can easily understand why the council fathers chose to see themselves in continuity with it. Unlike Trent, Vatican I issued a constitution on faith that included a chapter on revelation. Basically, revelation was seen as God's revealed truth, which was not dependent on human reason and which was entrusted to the church to safeguard and proclaim by its dogmas. Despite Vatican I's opposition to rationalism,* the council did acknowledge the role human reason plays in allowing humans to comprehend God's revealed truth preserved in the faith. The council had to adjourn early because of the Franco-Prussian War in Europe, so it never had a chance to completely finish its work.

Like Trent, Vatican I also had anathemas. Four condemnations were issued, and the tone is clearly an antimodern one, which saw dangers lurking in many modern concepts like evolution and rationalism. The concern was also to protect the church's definition of the limits of the biblical canon and the authority of the Bible as God's inspired word. The multiple references to Vatican I in *Dei Verbum* reinforce these basic perspectives. Thus, *Dei Verbum* also emphasizes the role of the Holy Spirit in safeguarding the truth of Scripture and affirms the church's duty and right to uphold this truth.

The following chart gives a succinct comparison of these three ecumenical councils with regard to the teaching on revelation.

Comparison of Trent, Vatican I, and Vatican II on Revelation

Trent	Vatican I	Vatican II
Fourth Session, 1546	Third Session, 1870	Fourth Period, 1965
Title: No formal title, but concerned acceptance of the sacred books and apostolic traditions, and the role of the Latin Vulgate and means of interpretation	**Title:** *Dei Filius* (Son of God) On Revelation	**Title:** *Dei Verbum* (Word of God) Dogmatic Constitution on Divine Revelation
Content: Revelation is not discussed as a separate topic; rather, two decrees set forth the following: • the definitive canon of Sacred Scripture for the church (46 books in the Old Testament; 27 books in the New Testament); • the priority of the Latin Vulgate; • the affirmation that God is the author of both Testaments, either by the preaching of Christ or the dictation of the Holy Spirit; • an emphasis on the church's definitive role in interpretation of the Scriptures and forbidding individual interpretation.	**Content:** Revelation is discussed in chapter 2 of the Dogmatic Constitution on the Catholic Faith, most of which reiterates the basic teaching on Scripture from the Council of Trent.	**Content:** A dogmatic constitution fully devoted to the topic of divine revelation, discussed in an introduction and six chapters, covering the topics of revelation itself, the transmission of revelation, the divine inspiration of Scripture, the interrelationship of the Old and New Testaments, and the pastoral role of the Scriptures in the life of the church.

Table continued on page 12

| Anathemas and restrictions placed within the context of the two decrees, including restricting what biblical texts, with notes and/or interpretations, printers may print | Supplemented by four anathemas: (1) Against those who deny that God can be known through human reason and the created order; (2) Against those who deny the necessity of learning about God and the importance of worshipping; (3) Against those who affirm human self-development rather than acknowledging that God elevates human beings to divine perfection; (4) Against those who deny the canonical authority of all the books of the Old and New Testaments. | No anathemas |

Reproduced with minor changes from Ronald D. Witherup, *Scripture:* Dei Verbum (New York/Mahwah, NJ: Paulist Press, 2006), 43.

Providentissimus Deus *(Nov. 18, 1893)*

Although Pope Leo XIII (1810–1903) is better known for his encyclical letter on social justice, *Rerum Novarum* (1891), his encyclical letter on biblical studies, *Providentissimus Deus*, also exercised broad influence. The pope basically wanted to address in a formal way the scientific and literary developments that were happening in the nineteenth century and that had clearly been impacting interpretation of the Bible. One should keep in mind that some of these developments were dramatic. The nineteenth century was, after all, a century of enormous scientific and industrial progress but also a time of doctrinal anxiety in the Catholic Church that would lead to the "antimodernism" of the early twentieth century (see modernism* in the glossary).

Archaeology was beginning to make inroads in the Holy Land, for instance, with ramifications for biblical studies. Moreover, knowledge of the ancient biblical languages—Hebrew, Aramaic, Greek, and cognate languages—was also blossoming. Then there were also studies of literary forms found in the Bible and in antiquity that were beginning to impact biblical interpretation. Leo XIII addressed all these in his rather cautious encyclical. Although he was worried about the negative impact of many "modern" ideas on church teaching, he also wanted to encourage Catholic scholars to take advantage of new developments that might aid the proper, and more sophisticated, interpretation of Scripture. Thus, his encyclical letter basically encouraged Catholic biblical scholars to take advantage of these new techniques and apply them judiciously in ways that would promote better comprehension of the biblical message among Catholics.

Divino Afflante Spiritu
(Sept. 30, 1943, Memorial of Saint Jerome)

Pope Pius XII, like his predecessors from the nineteenth and early twentieth centuries, also harbored some fears about modern developments and how they could negatively influence the faith. Yet when he wrote this encyclical on biblical studies, published on the feast of Saint Jerome, patron saint of biblical scholars, he took a rather nuanced and balanced position. On the one hand, he repeated the church's teaching about the truth of the Scriptures, their inspired nature, their usefulness for Catholic spiritual and moral teaching, and the role of the Holy Spirit as guarantor of truth.

The pope, on the other hand, also recognized the great potential in the modern sciences for aiding the better comprehension of the Scriptures as ancient documents. Thus, his encyclical encouraged Catholic scholars to use all the modern means available, such as archaeology, literary and linguistic studies, to explore the Scriptures and advance biblical exegesis.* This balanced approach finds its way into *Dei Verbum* and helped give the dogmatic constitution its refined orientation to the question of biblical interpretation.

Sancta Mater Ecclesia (Apr. 21, 1964)

A teaching of the Pontifical Biblical Commission that exercised a direct influence on the final formulation of *Dei Verbum* was *Sancta Mater Ecclesia*, the Instruction on the Historical Truth of the Gospels. Several points are noteworthy in this regard.

First, note that the instruction was issued in 1964, that is, while the council was still in process! Behind the scenes there had been many discussions going on among biblical experts, theologians, and council fathers over certain aspects of Scripture and how they would be addressed by the constitution being drafted. The Pontifical Biblical Commission, at that time a teaching arm of the Congregation for the Doctrine of the Faith, issued this instruction with an eye to helping give some direction to the council fathers.

The second point is that *Dei Verbum* actually adopts the literal title of the Biblical Commission document, for the first words of paragraph 19 in Latin are "Sancta Mater Ecclesia" (Holy Mother Church). One could hardly miss the affirmation that this implies in accepting the basic teaching of the Biblical Commission.

The third and most important point is the impact this document had. Its primary teaching, that the four canonical gospels themselves consist of three different levels of "tradition," and consequently are not necessarily eyewitness accounts of the ministry of Jesus of Nazareth, became enshrined in paragraph 19 of *Dei Verbum*, and later in the *Catechism of the Catholic Church* (126). The constitution explicitly acknowledges these three levels: the oral teaching of Jesus in history, the subsequent preaching of the apostles recounting the stories of Jesus, and the written testimony of the four evangelists who collected, organized, edited, and synthesized these oral and written traditions. This teaching explains why interpreters of the gospels must be careful to distinguish these levels of gospel tradition and not overstep the bounds of purely historical assertions. Note also, however, that *Dei Verbum* insists that this complex process of oral, written, and edited gospel traditions still preserves the "truth" of Scripture relating to Jesus and his teaching.

Finally, one can add that those who wish to affirm the literal historicity of the gospels in a way that denies this multilayered process do not have this option in Catholic teaching. Of course, the same paragraph of *Dei Verbum* affirms the basic historicity of the gospels. There is no room for asserting that they are fiction or simply made-up stories. They are based upon the ministry of Jesus. Over time, however, accretions crept into the text and the formulation of these traditions was influenced by developing Christian beliefs. One must always exercise caution when making historical claims about the "Jesus traditions," which is one reason why biblical scholars continue to research the gospels carefully for kernels of history that are embedded there.

Other Influences

Many other influences helped to shape *Dei Verbum* that are not noted on the chart, since I have only highlighted the most evident and important. For instance, many church fathers and theologians are quoted or cited (Augustine, Jerome, Ambrose, Irenaeus, John Chrysostom, Cyril of Jerusalem, etc.). There are also references to other councils of the church (Nicaea II, Fourth Council of Constance) and to the teachings of other popes (Pius XI, Benedict XV). Such citations are evidence that *Dei Verbum* should be seen in continuity with prior church tradition.

In addition, we should recall that several modern theologians marked the shape of the constitution and other council documents, most notably, Yves Congar (1904–95), Karl Rahner (1904–84), Henri de Lubac (1896–1991), Pierre Teilhard de Chardin (1881–1955), Hans Urs von Balthasar (1905–88), Louis Bouyer (1913–2004), Edward Schillebeeckx (1914–2009), Gérard Philips (1899–1972), Hans Küng (b. 1928), Joseph Ratzinger (b. 1927), and others. Several scholars from the so-called "Louvain school" (Belgium), such as Gérard Philips, made particularly significant contributions to *Dei Verbum* and other council documents. Many scholars exemplified the perspective of the so-called *nouvelle théologie** (French, "new theology" [see also theology* in the glossary]) that marked the European context so significantly by the middle of the twentieth century. The name "new theology" was given to this group of forward-thinking, French-speaking theologians in the 1940s—though they were not an organized group as such—in order to distinguish their progressive thought from the standard "Roman" theological approach (often called "manual" theology* for the use of textbooks or manuals of instruction) that had been in place for centuries. Many of these theologians functioned as official experts (Latin, *periti*) or advisors to bishops throughout the council, and several had a direct hand in shaping the language of council documents. Paradoxically, this was almost a rehabilitation of the "new theology," as it had earlier been condemned by Pope Pius XII's encyclical letter *Humani Generis* (1950) as dangerous! What marked the style of this "new theology" was called *ressourcement** (French, "going back to the sources"). It constituted a return to biblical, patristic, and medieval theological traditions that was to stamp much of the theology of Vatican II. Paradoxically again, revisiting the church's more ancient history in these earlier sources would significantly revitalize the church in the modern period.

We do not have the time or space to explore all these considerations in detail. The essential point is to understand the larger context out of which *Dei Verbum* was born. As with all church teachings, the constitution grew out of certain historical, cultural, and theological settings that helped to shape its final form. Part of the challenge and beauty of deepening our comprehension of this document is keeping such a rich background in mind.

CHAPTER TWO

A Brief Commentary on *Dei Verbum*

The purpose of this chapter is to give a brief commentary on the Dogmatic Constitution on Divine Revelation by summarizing the main teachings of each section of the document. Along the way we will make some specific observations on paragraphs that address crucial points. This process will be most effective if the reader directly consults the accompanying text of *Dei Verbum*, which precedes each brief section of comment. Footnotes in the text of *Dei Verbum* can be found gathered together at the end of this chapter. Note also that there are twenty-six numbered paragraphs to the constitution, but several of these contain additional unnumbered paragraphs. Each numbered paragraph is reproduced here in its entirety prior to the commentary on it. To facilitate the process, the text of *Dei Verbum* is fully indented and produced in a smaller font.

Prologue

Paragraph 1

Hearing the word of God reverently and proclaiming it confidently, this holy synod makes its own the words of St. John: "We proclaim to you the eternal life which was with the Father and was made manifest to us—that which we have seen and heard we proclaim also to you, so that you may have fellowship with us; and our fellowship is with the Father and with his Son Jesus Christ" (1 Jn 1:2-3). Following, then, in the steps of the councils of Trent and Vatican I, this synod wishes to set forth the authentic teaching on divine revelation and its transmission. For it wants the whole world to hear the summons to salvation, so that through hearing it may believe, through belief it may hope, through hope it may come to love.[1]

The short one-paragraph prologue gives the constitution its formal title, taken from the first two Latin words, *Dei Verbum*, "the word of God." It speaks of a twofold dynamic, hearing and proclaiming the word of God. It also quotes explicitly the beautiful passage from 1 John 1:2-3 that speaks of hearing and proclaiming the "eternal life" that comes from God in Jesus Christ. Although it is a short biblical passage, it touches many aspects of revelation* that the constitution goes on to address. Note too the emphasis on "hearing" the Word. It places the church in the more humble mode of receptivity prior to entering into evangelization or announcing the "Good News."

The prologue also explicitly references two previous church councils, Trent and Vatican I, whose teaching on revelation and its transmission serve as a foundation for the instruction taken up in the dogmatic constitution. This is not a minor point, since subsequent debates about the proper interpretation of *Dei Verbum* revolve around how much it is in continuity or discontinuity with prior church teaching. The council fathers clearly orient their teaching first in the direction of continuity with two of the church's most important recent councils.

Finally, the prologue speaks of the desire to proclaim the truth of revelation to the "whole world" and evokes a kind of chain reaction that the council fathers hope takes effect. They desire that hearing will lead to belief, belief to hope, and hope to love. This is evidence of the pastoral nature of this "dogmatic" teaching that is emblematic of the entire council.

The effect of the prologue is to make the constitution more an invitation to understanding what is ultimately a mystery, how God reveals himself for our salvation. It also subtly indicates that more will be involved than simply talking about Scripture, God's sacred word. The eternal spoken "Word of God" is first and foremost a person, the Word made flesh, Jesus Christ. He is the primary and full embodiment of God's revelation who is also encountered in the written Sacred Scriptures of the church.

After this eloquent prologue, the constitution launches directly into its main topic, divine revelation. Although the entire constitution is obviously essential Catholic teaching, the first three chapters can be said to be the "meat" of its teaching. These chapters directly tackle some of the most profound, mysterious, and thorny concepts in theology.

Chapter I: Divine Revelation Itself (pars. 2–6)

This first chapter comprises five rather dense paragraphs that describe in detail the concept of divine revelation *itself*. Its very biblical orientation is evident in the fact that it contains no fewer than thirty-two biblical citations in the text and notes.

Paragraph 2

> It pleased God, in his goodness and wisdom, to reveal himself and to make known the mystery of his will (see Eph 1:9), which was that people can draw near to the Father, through Christ the Word made flesh, in the Holy Spirit, and thus become sharers in the divine nature (see Eph 2:18; 2 Pet 1:4). By this revelation, then, the invisible God (see Col 1:15; 1 Tim 1:17), from the fullness of his love, addresses men and women as his friends (see Ex 33:11; Jn 15:14-15) and lives among them (see Bar 3:38), in order to invite and receive them into his own company. The pattern of this revelation unfolds through deeds and words which are intrinsically connected: works performed by God in the history of salvation show forth and confirm the doctrine and realities signified by the words; the words, for their part, proclaim the works, and bring to light the mystery they contain. The most intimate truth thus revealed about God and human salvation shines forth for us in Christ, who is himself both the mediator and the sum total of revelation.[2]

The first paragraph (2) of this chapter begins by putting the emphasis on God's initiative. Revelation is God's own desire. God *wills* to reveal himself to humanity and thus chose to make known the mystery of his divine intentions so that humanity, through Jesus Christ, would have free and unrestrained access to God. The language is carefully constructed. The term "mystery" (Latin, *sacramentum*) is very biblical, especially a key concept in the letters of Paul, one of which is referenced here (Eph 1:9), along with other Pauline citations throughout the paragraph.

This divine initiative, the text explains, is the invisible God making himself known visibly so that human beings might become friends of God. Revelation is thus a gracious act of loving friendship. God invites us to fellowship! This is a very personal concept that the paragraph labels the "pattern" (Latin, *oeconomia*) of revelation made up both of gestures and words seen throughout human history, as recounted especially in the biblical books. They demonstrate "the history of salvation," the incredible series of deeds and words that culminated in Christ himself, whom the text describes as both "the mediator and the sum total of revelation."

This paragraph, then, places revelation squarely in the arena of a divine mystery initiated by the grace of God, but that nonetheless can be discerned by human beings because there are concrete indicators, words and deeds, which find their apex in a person, the Word made flesh, Jesus Christ. These words (Latin, *verba*) and deeds (Latin, *gesta*, a more personalistic concept than *facta*) are intimately connected. The words and deeds of the Messiah are emblematic of God's activity throughout history.

Paragraph 3

> God, who creates and conserves all things by his Word (see Jn 1:3), provides constant evidence of himself in created realities (see Rom 1:19-20). Furthermore, wishing to open up the way to heavenly salvation, he manifested himself to our first parents from the very beginning. After the fall, he buoyed them up with the hope of salvation, by promising redemption (see Gen 3:15); and he has never ceased to take care of the human race, in order to give eternal life to all those who seek salvation by persevering in doing good (see Rom 2:6-7). In his own time, God called Abraham and made him into a great nation (see Gen 12:2-3). After the era of the patriarchs, he taught this nation, through Moses and the prophets, to recognize him as the only living and true God, as a provident Father and just judge. He taught them, too, to look for the promised Savior. And so, throughout the ages he prepared the way for the Gospel.

The next paragraph (3) of the chapter sets out to explain even further how this theological and christological drama takes place. God reveals himself in his Word—Christ, referring to John 1:3—but also through concrete evidence in all of creation, and especially through the history of salvation. Essentially, this paragraph offers a little synopsis of the biblical story. It begins with creation, then tells of the fall of Adam and Eve, the covenant with Abraham, the era of the patriarchs, the leadership of Moses, the preaching of the prophets, and ultimately the hope for and expectation of a Savior. Naturally, from the Christian perspective, this entire history, which is evidence of God's loving outreach to humanity, prepares for the Gospel message. In other words, the whole history of salvation leads to Christ, who is the specific focus of the next paragraph.

Paragraph 4

> After God had spoken many times and in various ways through the prophets, "in these last days he has spoken to us by a Son" (Heb 1:1-2). For he sent his Son, the eternal Word who enlightens all humankind, to live among them and tell them about the inner life of God (Jn 1:1-18). Hence, Jesus Christ, sent as "a man among men and women,"[3] "speaks the words of God" (Jn 3:34), and accomplishes the same work which the Father gave him to do (see Jn 5:36; 17:4). As a result, he himself—to see whom is to see the Father (see Jn 14:9)—completed and perfected revelation and confirmed it with divine guarantees. Everything to do with his presence and his manifestation of himself was involved in achieving this: his words and works, signs and miracles, but above all his death and glorious resurrection from the dead, and finally his sending of the Spirit of truth. He revealed that God was with us, to deliver us from the darkness of sin and death, and to raise us up to eternal life.
>
> The Christian dispensation, therefore, since it is the new and definitive covenant, will never pass away; and no new public revelation is to be expected before the glorious manifestation of our Lord Jesus Christ (1 Tim 6:14 and Tit 2:13).

Using a beautiful image from Hebrews that speaks of how the prophets prepared for the revelation of God's Son (Heb 1:1-2), this paragraph explains in various ways the significance of Christ as the epitome of God's revelation. Christ is the one who in fact reveals God most intimately and brings us into direct contact with God. The text cites several passages from John's gospel, the most incarnationally* oriented book of the New Testament because of its emphasis on Jesus, the Word made flesh, who pitches his tent in the midst of humanity (John 1:14). He is fully a man among human beings yet God's Son who reveals the Father to us. His "words and deeds" and his "signs and wonders," and most especially his death and resurrection, have confirmed that he is "perfected revelation" itself. He alone could reveal God's mysterious plan and fulfill the promise of salvation.

The final section concludes with a strong statement about the lasting power of this final revelation of God in Jesus Christ. It states that the "Christian dispensation," that is, the new and eternal covenant established by Jesus Christ, is the final, ultimate, and definitive act in revelation. There can be no better act to come. Christ is the summit of revelation. Thus, *Dei Verbum* explicitly states that "no new public revelation is to be expected." God's final Word has been spoken. The mediator and content of revelation are already known. He is Christ, God's own Son, who sends the Spirit for our aid and benefit. If we expect no further revelation, we nonetheless await the final act of salvation in this gracious divine drama of love, namely, Christ's glorious return at the end of time. In essence, Christ sums up everything about revelation, but there is more glory to come in eternal life.

Having spoken of God's outreach in Christ, the sum of revelation, the text now turns to the other side of the equation. If God is the primary actor in this divine drama, human beings nevertheless have a role to play. God's extended offer of fellowship demands a response. In the Christian dispensation, proclamation always requires response. So the focus now shifts to human responsibility in paragraph 5.

Paragraph 5

> "The obedience of faith" (see Rom 16:26; compare Rom 1:5; 2 Cor 10:5-6) must be our response to God who reveals. By faith one freely commits oneself entirely to God, making "the full submission of intellect and will to God who reveals,"[4] and willingly assenting to the revelation given by God. For this faith to be accorded we need the grace of God, anticipating it and assisting it, as well as the interior helps of the Holy Spirit, who moves the heart and converts it to God and opens the eyes of the mind and "makes it easy for all to accept and believe the truth."[5] The same Holy Spirit constantly perfects faith by his gifts, so that revelation may be more and more deeply understood.

The text immediately speaks of "the obedience of faith," an expression from Saint Paul cited in several passages from Paul's letters (esp. Rom 16:26). What God asks of us in response to his outreach is faithful obedience. We are asked to surrender ourselves totally to God, heart, mind, will, soul, all that we are. But God knows we are weak and need help in this response. So the text points out that we have the Holy Spirit as our guide. This was Christ's parting gift to the world. The Holy Spirit helps us in our interior life and enables us to better see God and to comprehend the mystery of revelation. Faith is thus both human response and free gift of the Holy Spirit. Indeed, the Spirit helps to perfect or bring to completion our faith.

Paragraph 6

> By divine revelation God wished to manifest and communicate both himself and the eternal decrees of his will concerning the salvation of humankind. He wished, in other words, "to share with us divine benefits which entirely surpass the powers of the human mind to understand."[6]
>
> The holy synod professes that "God, the first principle and last end of all things, can be known with certainty from the created world, by the natural light of human reason" (see Rom 1:20). It teaches that it is to his revelation that we must attribute the fact "that those things which in themselves are not beyond the grasp of human reason, can, in the present condition of the human race, be known by all with ease, with firm certainty, and without the contamination of error."[7]

The final numbered paragraph (6) of this chapter of the constitution returns to the question of the content of revelation, this time focusing on what faith demands of us in terms of belief. This section echoes the teaching of Vatican Council I, which is cited in the footnotes. God shares with us "divine benefits" (Latin, *bona divina*) that are beyond our full comprehension yet are also the object of faith and can be known even with our limited human minds. This assertion concerns revealed religious truths that can be known by human reason and "without the contamination of error," a concept we will address more fully below. This is so because the Holy Spirit is the guarantor of the faith, as was just stated in the previous numbered paragraph (5). The language of the text, however, in keeping with the general tone of the constitution, goes a bit beyond Vatican I because it is more personalistic, speaking of God's revelation as communicated and manifested (Latin, *communicare, manifestare*). This is decidedly more pastoral language.

As dense as this chapter of *Dei Verbum* is, it unfolds in a logical and comprehensive fashion. Revelation begins with God and ends with God. God is both the source and goal of revelation. Christ is the definitive revealer of this loving gesture, and by our obedient response of faith through the Holy Spirit, we show ourselves to be God's humble servants, the creatures God made us to be. At one and the same time, the constitution is theological (oriented toward God), christological (Christ-centered), and trinitarian (expressing the divine reality of Father, Son, and Spirit [see Trinity* in the glossary]).

Chapter II: The Transmission of Divine Revelation (pars. 7–10)

With the basic description of divine revelation concluded, *Dei Verbum* now turns to *how* this revelation is communicated or transmitted. This is the chapter that will openly broach the complex problem of the relationship between Scripture and tradition, a concept that led to open disagreements between Protestants and Catholics at the Reformation and its aftermath. Of the four paragraphs that comprise this chapter, the last two are particularly critical (9–10).

Paragraph 7

> God graciously arranged that what he had once revealed for the salvation of all peoples should last forever in its entirety and be transmitted to all generations. Therefore, Christ the Lord, in whom the entire revelation of the most high God is summed up (see 2 Cor 1:20; 3:16–4:6), having fulfilled in his own person and promulgated with his own lips the Gospel promised beforehand by the prophets, commanded the apostles to preach it to everyone as the source of all saving truth and moral law, communicating God's gifts to them.[8] This was faithfully done: it was done by the apostles who handed on, by oral preaching, by their example, by their dispositions, what they themselves had received—whether from the lips of Christ, from his way of life and his works, or by coming to know it through the prompting of the Holy Spirit; it was done by those apostles and others associated with them who, under the inspiration of the same Holy Spirit, committed the message of salvation to writing.[9]
>
> In order that the full and living Gospel might always be preserved in the church the apostles left bishops as their successors. They gave them "their own position of teaching authority."[10] This sacred tradition, then, and the sacred scripture of both Testaments, are like a mirror, in which the church, during its pilgrim journey here on earth, contemplates God, from whom it receives everything, until such time as it is brought to see him face to face as he really is (see 1 Jn 3:2).

The first sentence of the first numbered paragraph (7) orients the entire chapter with two essential concepts. God intended that his revelation about salvation would "last forever" among human beings in all its integrity and be "transmitted" or handed on to succeeding generations. This naturally leads to the role of the apostles, Christ's first followers, who were originally charged with bringing the Gospel or Good News to the world. He (Christ) who is both the summit and ultimate content of revelation sent out his apostles on mission. Thus God gives human beings the task to transmit the divine message faithfully.

The text also draws attention in footnotes to several passages from the Council of Trent. In essence, it summarizes the standard faith of the church that the apostles and their colleagues faithfully proclaimed the Gospel of Christ and handed on, by preaching orally and then in written fashion, what they themselves had received either from Christ himself or from the promptings of the Holy Spirit. The paragraph emphasizes the role of the Holy Spirit in faithfully preserving this tradition. Technically, we could say this is a pneumatological* (from Greek *pneuma*, "spirit" or "breath") emphasis that is characteristic of *Dei Verbum*. It is the Spirit whose inspiration guided the faithful writers of the Scriptures. Thus, one might conceive of the process of transmitting revelation in a *vertical* fashion, from the Spirit to the apostles and evangelists. But then to spread the Good News further, a *horizontal* means was also necessary, that is, the apostolic preaching passed on to succeeding generations of bishops and their successors in the church.

Dei Verbum thus sees the transmission of revelation as a faithful, unbroken chain of sacred communication. Christ entrusted the message to his apostles, who in turn entrusted it to their successors, and so on. This "tradition" (distinguished from human traditions) constitutes both the church's teaching *and* the Scriptures, both Old and New Testaments. There is a significant overlap in these concepts. Together Scripture and tradition give witness to the saving message of what God has done in Christ for humanity. The paragraph concludes with a lovely image of this tradition and Scripture functioning like a sacred "mirror" for the church. In them we see the invisible God whom one day we will meet face-to-face.

Three observations about this paragraph (7) are noteworthy. First, the language of handing on or "transmitting" the faith is very biblical itself. It was already used by Jews to speak of the faithful communication of the truths of God preserved for centuries both orally and in the sacred writings, the Hebrew Scriptures we now call the Old Testament. In the New Testament, this custom is also witnessed in the letters of Saint Paul, such as when he recalls traditions about the Lord's Supper (the Last Supper) and the resurrection that he had received and passed on to his communities (1 Cor 11:23-26; 15:1-8).

Second, the mention of "the pilgrim journey" of the church on earth is a key image from Vatican II. It harks back to *Lumen Gentium*, the Dogmatic Constitution on the Church (LG 48, 50). It is an image that runs counter to earlier images of the church as regal, domineering, victorious, exalted, triumphant, and, to some people, arrogant. As a group of pilgrims the church is seen in a more humble manner, on an eternal pilgrimage, journeying toward her final glory with God. In the meantime we remain totally reliant upon God's graciousness to lead us forward. The image of the pilgrim church in this section of *Dei Verbum* underscores our reliance upon revelation as pure grace, pure gift, which we are nonetheless charged to disseminate to the world.

Finally, on the complex topic of inspiration the constitution nowhere adopts a theory of how it works. Several theories have been proposed by scholars over the centuries. One could place them on a scale that runs from the full verbal inspiration of every word of the Bible to a broad concept of the inspiration of the "community of believers" who compiled the sacred texts as "inspired" books. The following chart shows several principal theories of inspiration, each of which has pros and cons.

The Spectrum of Theories of Biblical Inspiration

Theory	Description
Full Verbal Inspiration	Every word of the Bible is inspired, whether in the original language or in translation; tied to the notion of "inerrancy" and tends toward a literal, fundamentalist reading of Scripture
Limited Verbal Inspiration	The words of the Bible are inspired with regard to their religious message or faith perspective, but there is room for possible scientific or historical errors in the Bible that do not affect salvation
Inspiration of Content	Not tied to the inspiration of the actual words of Scripture, this theory emphasizes that the general "content" or "meaning" of the Bible is inspired

Inspiration of the Human Authors	Emphasizes that the human authors were inspired by God in what they wrote but the expression of their religious insights was put in fully human words
Inspiration of the Early Faith Community	Attempts to account for the lengthy and complex process of the formulation of the sacred canon of Scripture by emphasizing the general inspiration of the early Christians as a faith community rather than individual authors of the biblical books

Reproduced with minor changes from Ronald D. Witherup, *Scripture:* Dei Verbum (Mahwah, NJ: Paulist Press, 2006), 90.

Dei Verbum sidesteps such theories and simply asserts the *fact* of inspiration without explaining how it works. Since this is indeed a difficult area to resolve, the council fathers were probably exercising prudence in not wanting to limit an ongoing technical discussion of this very complex issue.

Paragraph 8

Thus, the apostolic preaching, which is expressed in a special way in the inspired books, was to be preserved in a continuous line of succession until the end of time. Hence the apostles, in handing on what they themselves had received, warned the faithful to maintain the traditions which they had learned either by word of mouth or by letter (see 2 Th 2:15), and to fight for the faith that had been handed on to them once and for all (see Jude 3).[11] What was handed on by the apostles comprises everything that serves to make the people of God live their lives in holiness and increase their faith. In this way the church, in its doctrine, life and worship, perpetuates and transmits to every generation all that it itself is, all that it believes.

The tradition that comes from the apostles makes progress in the church, with the help of the Holy Spirit.[12] There is a growth in insight into the realities and words that are being passed on. This comes about through the contemplation and study of believers who ponder these things in their hearts (see Lk 2:19 and 51). It comes from the intimate sense of spiritual realities which they experience. And it comes from the preaching of those who, on succeeding to the office of bishop, have received the sure charism of truth. Thus, as the centuries go by, the church is always advancing towards the plenitude of divine truth, until eventually the words of God are fulfilled in it.

The sayings of the church Fathers are a witness to the life-giving presence of this tradition, showing how its riches are poured out in the practice and life of the believing and praying church. By means of the same tradition, the full canon of the sacred books is known to the church and the holy scriptures themselves are more thoroughly understood and constantly made effective in the church. Thus God, who spoke in the past, continues to converse with the spouse of his beloved Son. And the Holy Spirit, through whom the living voice of the Gospel rings out in the church—and through it in the world—leads believers to the full truth and makes the word of Christ dwell in them in all its richness (see Col 3:16).

The next paragraph (8), which comprises three sections, then turns to examine a key concept that paradoxically was never treated by earlier councils in any systematic or thorough way—tradition. The text approaches the complex notion of tradition from three different angles.

The first topic summarizes the "apostolic preaching" that had begun at Jesus' command and that is found preserved in the Sacred Scriptures. The apostles got the ball rolling, as it were, by passing on orally and later in writing what they themselves had received. This is the great chain of tradition. The purpose of the tradition is to preserve the message of revelation, to make the faith grow, and to foster holiness among "the people of God" (another biblical image for the church from *Lumen Gentium*, chap. 2). Thus tradition begins with the *preservation* of what has been received from God.

The next step, however, reveals a second angle on tradition. This apostolic tradition did not simply remain stagnant but expanded in such a way that there was "growth in insight into the realities and words" of revelation. The paragraph particularly underlines the importance of study, reflection, and religious experience (such as in liturgy) over time, under the Holy Spirit's guidance, as helping to shape the apostolic tradition. This is a critical point, for sometimes Catholics mistakenly believe the faith has never changed. While the content of the faith remains constant, its comprehension and expression have grown over the centuries. Tradition thus has a *dynamic* aspect to it. It is a living reality. The formulation and comprehension of the divine mysteries can grow over time, all under guidance of the Holy Spirit. Pope John XXIII spoke eloquently of the need for a fresh approach to church tradition when he convoked the council at its opening:

> What is needed is that this certain and immutable doctrine,* to which the faithful owe obedience, be studied afresh and reformulated in contemporary terms. For this deposit* of faith, or truths which are contained in our time-honored teaching is one thing; the manner in which these truths are set forth (with their meaning preserved intact) is something else. (*Gaudet Mater Ecclesia*, Opening Address, Oct. 11, 1962)

He was thus not calling for new doctrines or dogmas, but for new and timely formulations of them that would rejuvenate the church. He used the Italian word *aggiornamento** ("updating") to express his vision of making the church's teaching more understandable today. How does this process of deepening our comprehension happen? *Dei Verbum* here gives three main examples: contemplation, study, and the preaching of those so charged by ordination, especially the bishops.

Even more importantly, the third angle on tradition expressed in the next (unnumbered) section highlights the roles of the church fathers, the liturgy and prayer life of the church, and the Sacred Scriptures themselves in the transmission of revelation. The Holy Spirit is again referenced as the one who guides this process. Under this sacred guidance, the tradition of the church is not merely something ancient and simply to be maintained. Rather, the text speaks of the "life-giving" tradition and "the living voice of the Gospel." These concepts underscore the fact that tradition is constantly being utilized, applied, and actualized in a variety of ways as the church moves toward its final destiny with God. On her pilgrim path the church also speaks out to the world, passing on the sacred tradition in fulfillment of Jesus' instruction to the apostles. So the great chain of tradition continues unbroken in the life of the church. It is a living and life-giving reality.

These three angles on tradition having been described, the constitution turns its attention in the next paragraph to an even more complex question—the relationship between Scripture and tradition.

Paragraph 9

> Sacred tradition and sacred scripture, then, are bound closely together, and communicate one with the other. Flowing from the same divine well-spring, both of them merge, in a sense, and move towards the same

goal. Sacred scripture is the utterance of God put down as it is in writing under the inspiration of the Holy Spirit. And tradition transmits in its entirety the word of God which has been entrusted to the apostles by Christ the Lord and the Holy Spirit; it transmits it to the successors of the apostles so that, enlightened by the Spirit of truth, they may faithfully preserve, expound and disseminate it by their preaching. Thus it is that the church does not draw its certainty about all revealed truths from the holy scriptures alone. Hence, both scripture and tradition must be accepted and honored with equal devotion and reverence.[13]

In this paragraph (9) the delicate and complex question of the relationship between Scripture and tradition comes front and center. That the council fathers would broach this topic at Vatican II after some four hundred years of verbal battles between Protestants and Catholics, who defined this very issue differently, shows the boldness of the vision of the council. But as we will see, the constitution does not finally resolve *all* the complexities surrounding this problem.

The first statement of paragraph 9 simply states that Scripture and tradition are closely connected and involved in mutual communication. Right away this signals that Catholics cannot say they simply hold on to tradition without Scripture. Nor can they say they hold to Scripture without tradition. As the text says, they flow from "the same divine well-spring." The two go hand in hand. But how? Three basic statements summarize the approach of the constitution:

(1) Both Scripture and tradition come from the same source (i.e., God).

(2) Scripture is the word of God written under the guidance of the Holy Spirit.

(3) Tradition takes the word of God and preserves it through the apostles and their successors, who are also under the guidance of the same Holy Spirit.

The obvious conclusion is then drawn. The church does not rely on Scripture alone, something that many Protestant denominations claim. Both Scripture and tradition are to be accepted, honored, and reverenced. (But remember: tradition is not merely a compilation of human customs but the accumulated wisdom of church teaching and scriptural reflection throughout history. There is an overlap in both concepts.)

The next paragraph (10), also with three sections, attempts to clarify this relationship between Scripture and tradition even further.

Paragraph 10

Tradition and scripture make up a single sacred deposit of the word of God, which is entrusted to the church. By adhering to it the entire holy people, united to its pastors, remains always faithful to the teaching of the apostles, to the communion of life, to the breaking of bread and the prayers (see Acts 2:42, Greek text). So, in maintaining, practicing and professing the faith that has been handed on there is a unique interplay between the bishops and faithful.[14]

But the task of getting an authentic interpretation of the word of God, whether in its written form or in the form of tradition,[15] has been entrusted to the living teaching office of the church alone.[16] Its authority in this matter is exercised in the name of Jesus Christ. This magisterium is not superior to the word of God, but is rather its servant. It teaches only what has been handed on to it. At the divine command and with the help of the Holy Spirit, it listens to this devoutly, guards it reverently and expounds it faithfully. All that it proposes for belief as being divinely revealed it draws from this sole deposit of faith.

It is clear, therefore, that, in the supremely wise arrangement of God, sacred tradition, sacred scripture and the magisterium of the church are so connected and associated that one of them cannot stand without the others. Working together, each in its own way under the action of the one Holy Spirit, they all contribute effectively to the salvation of souls.

This numbered paragraph (10) begins with another bold assertion. Lest one think of Scripture and tradition as two separate sources of revelation, *Dei Verbum* says explicitly that they "make up a single sacred deposit of the word of God" entrusted to the church! This is important because Vatican Council I had seemingly emphasized two sources of revelation. Remember that the fathers of Vatican II had rejected the first draft of the constitution on revelation entirely. Its title had harked back to Vatican I and *implied* two sources of revelation. Here the council makes it quite clear that Scripture and tradition belong together, and together they constitute one *source* of revelation. Yet note that the words "sacred deposit" (Latin, *sacrum depositum*) are also used. Although the constitution has emphasized the personal nature of divine revelation up to this point, there is also *content* to revelation. There is a deposit of divine truths that have been entrusted to the church and to which all the faithful are asked to adhere (see 1 Tim 6:20; 2 Tim 1:14). Bishops and faithful alike are asked to practice, profess, and adhere to this faith. The example from the Acts of the Apostles is given wherein the early church preserved the teaching of the apostles, fostered fellowship, and "broke the bread," that is, celebrated Eucharist together (Acts 2:42, Greek text).

The final movement in this chapter of *Dei Verbum* advances the discussion even further in trying to clarify how the church remains faithful to the transmission of the revelation she has received from God. Since both Scripture and tradition have been entrusted to the church, the text says Christ gave the church authority (Latin, *auctoritas*) to exercise control over this deposit in Christ's name. Here the constitution introduces the concept of the *magisterium* (= living teaching office) of the church. This is the church's power and authority to teach and maintain the faith authentically, under the guidance of the Holy Spirit and in the name of Jesus Christ. But *Dei Verbum* then says something quite remarkable: "This magisterium is not superior to the word of God, but is rather its servant. It teaches only what has been handed on to it . . . it listens to this devoutly, guards it reverently and expounds it faithfully." This is indeed a startling image. To see the magisterium as not superior to or above the word of God but as its servant orients the magisterium's authority and power in terms of service, not lording it over people. Yes, the constitution clearly indicates that only the magisterium of the church can authentically interpret the Scriptures, but this power is to be exercised as a servant, one who also *hears* the Word as all believers must hear it, in order to teach it authentically. This is reminiscent of Jesus' own teaching to his disciples that they are to be servants rather than masters (Mark 9:35; 10:42-45; Matt 20:25-28). Authority in the church is to be exercised with humility. Thus the magisterium is to serve the deposit of the faith under the Holy Spirit's guidance.

The final section of this detailed discussion of Scripture and tradition in paragraph 10 then seemingly throws a wrench into the discussion. It speaks of Scripture, tradition, and magisterium (teaching authority) as if they were almost three distinct realities, which nonetheless are God's "supremely wise arrangement" and work together for the salvation of souls. The text says that they "are so connected and associated that one of them cannot stand without the others. Working together, each in its own way under the action of the one Holy Spirit, they all contribute effectively to the salvation of souls."

How does one make sense of this very important paragraph 10 on Scripture and tradition? First, we must remember that the church had never before tried to clarify in any detail this issue. Theologians through the centuries have debated these questions, and the Protestant Reformation brought it to the fore with the unfortunate consequence of increasing the divide between Protestants and Catholics in ways that were caricatured by both groups. Catholics frequently identified magisterium and tradition as one and the same reality. They are not. Tradition is a much grander concept and is much larger than the teaching authority of the church. Furthermore, it must be remembered that the canon of Scriptures ultimately came from a formal declaration by the church (that is, its teaching authority) about what books were or were not inspired, and thus what were the limits of the canon. So, one cannot think of Scripture independently from the tradition. Indeed, perhaps one can conceive of them in a circular fashion in which the Word gives shape to the tradition, which in turn is defined by the magisterium, which declared the limit of the Scriptures, and so on. It is a bit like the chicken and the egg. They are intimately related, but which actually came first? In any case, of course, God, through the Holy Spirit, is the source. But there is a certain circularity to this complex relationship. In one sense, the Scriptures gave birth to the tradition; they bestow on the church its apostolic and missionary identity. In another sense, though, the tradition of the church brought the Scriptures into being by forming the canon of Sacred Scriptures. It was the church, acting under the guidance of the Holy Spirit, that ultimately determined what books belonged in the Bible and what ones were not authentically inspired writings, and thus to be excluded. This paradoxical circular reality constitutes part of the mystery of the relationship between Scripture and tradition. Both find their source in the Holy Spirit.

Second, the council's formulation avoided a thorny issue of the "material sufficiency"* of Scripture, that is, how much of revelation is contained in the content of the Scriptures themselves, whether Scripture or tradition has precedence, and to what degree the tradition of the church adds to revelation. These are complex issues that theologians have debated without final resolution, and *Dei Verbum* does not deal with these questions, seemingly because many bishops were reluctant to try to resolve such matters that were still being hotly debated among theological experts.

Third, as the 2008 synod* of bishops on the word of God pointed out—echoed later by Pope Benedict XVI's 2010 postsynodal apostolic exhortation *Verbum Domini*—this issue of the relationship between Scripture, tradition, and magisterium needs further work, as does the very concept of inspiration. (See chapter 3 of this book below for more information.) *Dei Verbum*, despite the tremendous strides it made in advancing the understanding of such a complex issue, did not resolve all the tensions that exist. One father of the council later suggested that the church needed to take to heart more *Dei Verbum*'s notion that the magisterium is the servant of the word of God, not its master. Abbot Christopher Butler, OSB, a *peritus* at the council and later a bishop, stated,

> It is all very well for us to say and believe that the magisterium is subject to Holy Scripture. But is there anybody who is in a position to tell the magisterium: Look, you are not practicing your subjection to Scripture in your teaching. (R. D. Witherup, *Scripture:* Dei Verbum, 99 and 140, n. 8)

The tension between the magisterium as, at one and the same time, both authentic interpreter of Scripture and its humble servant remains a contemporary challenge for church authorities.

Finally, we must remember too that *Dei Verbum* teaches—consistent with earlier church teaching—that, unlike other denominations, the Catholic Church has a magisterium that can definitively interpret Scripture when needed. But the church rarely exercises this power. The church is too wise to think that it should define what every passage of Scripture means. More often, the church has defined what a few passages do *not* mean rather than what they *do* mean. The prime example is the identity of the "brothers and sisters" of Jesus referred to in Mark 6:3. Unlike Protestants, the Catholic Church has definitively taught that they are not blood siblings of Jesus. Yet the church does not define exactly who they are, preferring to understand them as other relatives of Jesus in accord with an Old Testament tradition (see the *Catechism of the Catholic Church* 500).

The upshot of this discussion is that *Dei Verbum* has given the church a lot of rich food for thought on such delicate issues, but it also left to future generations some homework. As the church moves forward, doubtless there will be further advances on how to understand Scripture, tradition, and magisterium. Most important is to acknowledge that a Catholic approach always involves Scripture and tradition and not merely one or the other. Both are exercised in the authority of the magisterium and under the guidance of the Holy Spirit.

Chapter III: Sacred Scripture: Its Divine Inspiration and Its Interpretation (pars. 11–13)

Dei Verbum now turns its attention to a topic that had been mentioned already several times but not fully addressed, namely, divine inspiration of Scripture. These three numbered paragraphs occasioned considerable debate among the council fathers because the issue of *how* divine inspiration works had been, and remains, a complicated and not fully resolved issue. (At this writing, the concept is under discussion by the Pontifical Biblical Commission at the request of Pope Benedict XVI.)

Paragraph 11

> Those things revealed by God which are contained and presented in the text of sacred scripture have been written under the inspiration of the Holy Spirit. For holy mother church, relying on the faith of the apostolic age, accepts as sacred and canonical the books of the Old and the New Testaments, whole and entire, with all their parts, on the grounds that, written under the inspiration of the Holy Spirit (see Jn 20:31; 2 Tim 3:16; 2 Pet 1:19-21; 3:15-16), they have God as their author, and have been handed on as such to the church itself.[17] To compose the sacred books, God chose certain men who, all the while he employed them in this task, made full use of their powers and faculties[18] so that, though he acted in them and by them,[19] it was as true authors that they consigned to writing whatever he wanted written, and no more.[20]
>
> Since, therefore, all that the inspired authors, or sacred writers, affirm should be regarded as affirmed by the Holy Spirit, we must acknowledge that the books of scripture, firmly, faithfully and without error, teach that truth which God, for the sake of our salvation, wished to see confided to the sacred scriptures.[21] Thus "all Scripture is inspired by God, and is useful for teaching, for reproof, for correction and for training in righteousness, so that everyone who belongs to God may be proficient, equipped for every good work" (2 Tim 3:16-17, Greek text).

This first numbered paragraph (11) of chapter 3 of *Dei Verbum* can be divided into two sections. The first section affirms that the Sacred Scriptures—all of them, Old and New Testaments in their entirety—were composed under "the inspiration" of the Holy Spirit. Thus, God is their true "author." At the same time, God used certain individuals, the various biblical authors of both Testaments, as instruments for this divine composition. Even though God is the ultimate author, the biblical writers are also "true authors" because they used all their human skills and knowledge to record the message God "wanted written, and no more." The Scriptures, then, contain no less than the word of God, but also no more. This first section cites, among other traditions, Vatican Council I and several New Testament passages where the process of inspiration is at least alluded to, if not explicitly stated. We note the careful balance in this formulation. God is the author, but God worked through real human authors with all their talents and limitations, writing in accordance with the methods and means they knew. The constitution will come back to this point shortly.

The second section then turns to the quality of this composition. These writings, precisely because they are divinely inspired, "firmly, faithfully and without error, teach that truth which God, for the sake of our salvation, wished to see confided to the sacred scriptures." This is a key phrase. On the one hand, it acknowledges the lack of error in Scripture with regard to what it teaches *for the sake of salvation*. This is an affirmation that the Scriptures faithfully contain God's word without error (Latin, *sine errore*). On the other hand, the council deliberately avoided the language of *inerrancy* in the literal and global sense of that term, a characteristic of the approach of biblical fundamentalists who read the Scriptures literally and admit no errors, even scientific or historical, in the Bible. Note also that the document uses the singular "truth" rather than the plural "truths" in this context. The singular emphasizes the larger concept of what is necessary for salvation rather than focusing on individual church teachings.

This affirmation of *Dei Verbum*, then, is more nuanced than some might think. This is not a blanket approval of literal *inerrancy* but acknowledgment of the lack of errors regarding the essentials for salvation. From a modern perspective, it is well known that the Bible contains some scientific and historical errors, but none of these endanger the faith or delimit the truth of the Scriptures. The fact is that God, as the ultimate author of Scripture, had to rely on the human authors. In addition to their personal talents and limitations, in the course of the transmission of the Scriptures, simple historical or scientific errors inevitably crept into some of the Scriptures. In addition, the human authors were at the mercy of their respective cultures and the limits of human knowledge at the time. None of this in any way dilutes the truth of God's word. The section concludes with a quotation from Saint Paul, one of the few instances in Scripture where inspiration is forthrightly mentioned (2 Tim 3:16-17, Greek text). Paul's cited text also resounds with a pastoral implication, for it speaks of the usefulness of Scripture for teaching, reproof, and correction.

The next paragraph (12) proceeds in several sections to address the complicated question of divine inspiration.

Paragraph 12

Seeing that, in sacred scripture, God speaks through human beings in human fashion,[22] it follows that interpreters of sacred scripture, if they are to ascertain what God has wished to communicate to us, should carefully search out the meaning which the sacred writers really had in mind, that meaning which God had thought well to manifest through the medium of their words.

In determining the intention of the sacred writers, attention must be paid, among other things, to *literary genres*. The fact is that truth is differently presented and expressed in the various types of historical writing, in prophetical and poetical texts, and in other forms of literary expression. Hence the exegete must look for that meaning which the sacred writers, in given situations and granted the circumstances of their time and culture, intended to express and did in fact express, through the medium of a contemporary literary form.[23] Rightly to understand what the sacred authors wanted to affirm in their work, due attention must be paid both to the customary and characteristic patterns of perception, speech and narrative which prevailed in their time, and to the conventions which people then observed in their dealings with one another.[24]

But since sacred scripture must be read and interpreted with its divine authorship in mind,[25] no less attention must be devoted to the content and unity of the whole of scripture, taking into account the tradition of the entire church and the analogy of faith, if we are to derive their true meaning from the sacred texts. It is that task of exegetes to work, according to these rules, towards a better understanding and explanation of the meaning of sacred scripture in order that their research may help the church's judgment to mature. For, of course, all that has been said about the manner of interpreting scripture is ultimately subject to the judgment of the church which exercises the divinely conferred commission and ministry of watching over and interpreting the word of God.[26]

This numbered paragraph (12) attempts to explore the concept of inspiration further not by describing *how* it operates, which in fact is never addressed, but by laying out the boundaries with which one should approach Scripture. Because the Scriptures have two authors in a sense, God and the human writers, and because both have a hand in the process, the careful interpreter necessarily must pay close attention to both realities. This is simply an acknowledgment that the Scriptures are at one and the same time God's word in the form of human words.

We can consider this the "incarnational" understanding of Scripture. To grasp the meaning of the sacred text, one must try to understand the mind of the author. What was intended when such and such was written?

This is why the next (unnumbered) section of this paragraph explains further the need to pay close attention to the literary forms used by the ancient authors and to understand their times and their cultures. This is an explicit recognition that the ancient authors used the oral and literary means at their disposal to record the divine message. God did not hand them the finished Scriptures on a golden platter. The sacred authors used poetry, narrative, legal material, letters, parables, metaphors, similes, miracle stories, prayers, and so on in ways characteristic of their times. These are the "literary forms" referenced in the text. In essence, one does not read the Psalms in the same way one reads Paul's letters or the historical books of the Old Testament. One must pay attention to the human dimensions of the sacred texts. This section also implicitly upholds the importance of context for biblical interpretation. The historical contexts and methods of the biblical authors help shed light on the Scriptures and cannot be glossed over.

A little side comment is in order here. Since the time of the council, biblical scholars have reflected in depth on the issue of "authorial intention," that is, how one can know the intentions of ancient authors long deceased. Today, we recognize that these intentions are hidden forever. Scholars now speak of the "intentional fallacy,"* pointing out that we cannot really know what was intended since we cannot read their minds. We cannot, after all, ask the long-deceased ancient authors what they meant to say! What remains, however, are the ancient texts themselves. Thus, the process of interpretation itself is the best indicator we can have of what may have been the original intentions of the human authors of Scripture. A Catholic approach has already recognized boundless levels of meaning in the Scriptures (the "spiritual" or "theological" meanings), so that finally arriving at only one intentional meaning in the text is not the goal of interpretation. These and other complex issues were not recognized at the time of *Dei Verbum*. They are topics that have been addressed to some degree in subsequent church documents after the council, as noted in chapter 3 of this book below.

The next section of paragraph 12 immediately returns to the divine dimensions of the text. Catholic interpreters (professional exegetes) do not just observe the human qualities of the Scriptures but also read and interpret them in a larger context. *Dei Verbum* points to three principles from this larger context, which later get enshrined in the *Catechism of the Catholic Church* (2nd ed., 112–14):

> (1) Pay attention "to the content and unity of the whole Scripture."
>
> (2) "Read the Scripture 'within the living Tradition of the whole church.'"
>
> (3) Mind the "analogy of faith," that is, the "coherence" of teaching of the faith.

One might call this the safeguard of the Catholic method of interpreting the Bible. Interpretation does not take place in a vacuum. It is not the sole domain of professional biblical scholars. The constitution rightly encourages exegetes to do their work diligently, but it also exhorts them to do this in the context of the church's larger, living tradition. Paragraph 12 thus concludes by reiterating a principle enunciated in paragraph 10 of *Dei Verbum*. Ultimately, wherever questions of interpretation remain open-ended or highly disputed, the "judgment of the church" is the ultimate authority to resolve the matter definitively, if necessary. The text calls it the "ministry [Latin, *ministerio*] of watching over and interpreting the word of God."

The next and final paragraph (13) of this chapter is very short but expresses an important outlook that has been subtly present throughout the argumentation.

Paragraph 13

> Hence, in sacred scripture, without prejudice to God's truth and holiness, the marvelous "condescension" of eternal wisdom is plain to be seen, "that we may come to know the ineffable loving-kindness of God and see for ourselves the thought and care he has given to accommodating his language to our nature."[27] Indeed the words of God, expressed in human language, are in every way like human speech, just as the Word of the eternal Father, when he took on himself the weak flesh of human beings, became like them.

This final paragraph (13) sums up the teaching of the entire chapter by quoting a passage from Saint John Chrysostom (AD 347–407), one of the most skilled exegetes in church history. It describes God's graciousness in adapting his divine message through human instruments so that we could understand these teachings more clearly within our human limitations. The text also affirms that none of this "marvelous 'condescension'" mars the effectiveness of the word of God. Although the human expression remains, the divine message shines through. The constitution then returns to the incarnational principle it had used earlier, but this time explicitly invoking the analogy of the incarnation. Just as Jesus Christ was the Word made flesh, equally God and equally man, so Sacred Scripture is fully God's word in human words. Maintaining this balance is not easy. People are tempted often to collapse Jesus' humanity into his divinity. He is *God*, thus neglecting his humanity. Likewise, people sometimes allow the notion of divine Scriptures to overwhelm the human aspects of the Bible. It is *God's word*, thus forgetting the human words. (Like a bumper sticker I saw: "God said it; I believe it; that settles it!" Would that it were that simple!) Not to maintain this balance, however, leads one down the path of heresy, as church history has shown. By using such a compelling incarnational analogy, *Dei Verbum* challenges biblical interpreters to maintain the equilibrium carefully.

With the end of chapter 3 *Dei Verbum* concludes the most abstract and deeply theological discussion of divine revelation. The final three chapters will address more concrete topics that directly impact the pastoral life of the church. This is not to minimize them but simply to note the shift in focus.

Chapter IV: The Old Testament (pars. 14–16)

This chapter, which is usually seen as the weakest of the constitution, turns its attention in three short paragraphs to the role of the Old Testament in revelation. This is not a minor theme. Since the time of the heretic Marcion (ca. AD 85–ca. 165), many Christians mistakenly have overlooked or even rejected the Old Testament, thinking that it represents a bygone era or an outdated and non-Christian view of God. The constitution corrects any such notions by clearly laying out the essential role played by the Old Testament in preparing and setting the foundations for the New Testament. In fact, the New Testament cannot be properly understood apart from the Old Testament.

Paragraph 14

In his great love God intended the salvation of the entire human race. In preparation for this, in a special undertaking, he chose for himself a people to whom he would entrust his promises. By his covenant with Abraham (see Gen 15:18) and, through Moses, with the race of Israel (see Ex 24:8), he acquired a people for himself, and to them he revealed himself in words and deeds as the one, true, living God. It was his strategy that Israel might learn by experience God's ways with humanity and by listening to the voice of God speaking to them through the prophets might gradually understand his ways more fully and more clearly, and make them more widely known among the nations (see Ps 21[22]:28-29; 95:1-3; Is 2:1-4; Jer 3:17). The plan of salvation, foretold, recounted and explained by the sacred authors, appears as the true word of God in the books of the Old Testament, which is why these books, divinely inspired, retain a lasting value: "For whatever was written in former days was written for our instruction, so that by steadfastness and by the encouragement of the scriptures we might have hope" (Rom 15:4).

The first numbered paragraph (14) of chapter 4 gives a kind of shorthand version of the history of salvation. It explains the mystery of divine election, how God chose a certain people (ancient Israel) to be specially designated instruments out of loving concern for the whole human race. Though the Jews are not explicitly mentioned, there is no question they are this chosen people. They are "the race of Israel." This expresses the mystery of divine election. Even for the people of Israel this divine election was seen as extraordinary and mysterious. The Old Testament explains that God's choice of Israel was not because of some special quality of theirs but out of pure love (Deut 7:6-8). So the constitution recounts God's gracious act of making covenants with Israel, explicitly referencing Abraham (Gen 15:18) and Moses (Exod 24:8).

By these covenants God revealed himself to Israel as the "one, true, living God" in order that Israel would help make God known among the nations. Thus there was an ultimate universal dimension to this divine election. This is explained as a prophetic action, because the prophets of the Old Testament would be the source of preparing for the coming of the Messiah. The constitution refers to "the plan of salvation"—the divine plan (Latin, *oeconomia*) for how God would relate to human beings in the course of time and history. The purpose of the Old Testament as "divinely inspired" writings, it explains, was to foretell and prepare this divine drama of love. The paragraph then concludes with a wonderful quotation from Paul's letter to the Romans that shows the ongoing value of these Scriptures: "For whatever was written previously was written for our instruction, that by endurance and by the encouragement of the scriptures we might have hope" (Rom 15:4). Obviously, this quotation supports the church's understanding that the Scriptures exist ultimately for our spiritual benefit and constitute a most important means through which God communicates his will to human beings.

Paragraph 15

> The primary objective of the plan and lay-out of the Old Testament was that it should prepare for and declare in prophecy the coming of Christ, universal redeemer, and of the messianic kingdom (see Lk 24:44; Jn 5:39; 1 Pet 1:10), and should indicate it by means of various foreshadowing signs and symbols (see 1 Cor 10:11). For in the context of the human situation before the era of salvation established by Christ, the books of the Old Testament provide an understanding of God and humanity and make clear to all how a just and merciful God deals with humankind. These books, even though they contain matters which are imperfect and provisional, nevertheless contain authentic divine teaching.[28] Christians should accept with reverence these writings, which express a lively sense of God, which are a storehouse of sublime teaching on God and of sound wisdom on human life, as well as a wonderful treasury of prayers; in them, too, the mystery of our salvation is implicitly present.

This next paragraph (15) of *Dei Verbum* picks up with the concept of the divine plan and explains the prophetic value of the Old Testament in both preparing for the coming of the Messiah and his kingdom and explaining how God relates to humanity. By his gracious outreach, God is shown as the "just and merciful" author of creation. Then a striking admission is made. The text asserts the limitations of the Old Testament: "These books, even though they contain matters which are imperfect and provisional, nevertheless contain authentic divine teaching." This is actually a balanced assessment, as the next sentence shows. The constitution insists that these books of the Old Testament should be reverenced by Christians because, in and of themselves, they contain much wisdom and hold a "wonderful treasury of prayers" that are valid for all time. The conclusion is simple. The Old Testament holds the mystery of salvation, albeit in a hidden fashion that needs to be unraveled in order to be fully understood. Yet the Old Testament is here valued for its own sake as well as for its role in illuminating the New Testament.

The concluding paragraph (16) of this chapter comes back to the theme of the inspiration of the Scriptures. God is their true source.

Paragraph 16

> God, the inspirer and author of the books of both Testaments, in his wisdom has so brought it about that the New should be hidden in the Old and that the Old should be made manifest in the New.[29] For, although Christ founded the New Covenant in his blood (see Lk 22:20; 1 Cor 11:25), nevertheless the books of the Old Testament, all of them given a place in the preaching of the Gospel,[30] attain and display their full meaning in the New Testament (see Mt 5:17; Lk 24:27; Rom 16:25-26; 2 Cor 3:14-16) and, in their turn, shed light on it and explain it.

This final paragraph (16) of this chapter explains that God is the true inspirer and author of both the Old and New Testaments. Here the constitution resolves the tension between the Testaments by relying on an ancient principle enunciated by Saint Augustine (AD 354–430), one of the greatest theologians of church history. His principle is noted with these words: "the books of the Old Testament, all of them given a place in the preaching of the Gospel, attain and display their full meaning in the New Testament . . . and, in their turn, shed light on it and explain it." Various citations from the New Testament are put forth to uphold this proclamation. In no uncertain terms, the chapter's conclusion makes clear that the new covenant established in the blood of Christ was prepared for by all the previous covenants God had made with ancient Israel.

Note the two-way direction of this principle. The New is hidden in the Old so that it can be manifest in the New, but the New also sheds light on the Old so that it can be better understood in its full significance. Thus, the perpetual value of the Old Testament is set forth as a Catholic principle in this section of *Dei Verbum*. A later church teaching, The Jewish People and Their Sacred Scriptures in the Christian Bible, issued by the Pontifical Biblical Commission in 2002, would go on to explain in much more detail what *Dei Verbum* asserts in this chapter in rather brief form.

The next chapter of *Dei Verbum* then turns, in greater detail, to the New Testament.

Chapter V: The New Testament (pars. 17–20)

Having clarified the role of the Old Testament, the constitution in chapter 5 turns to the New Testament. A bit longer, with four numbered paragraphs (17–20), this chapter begins with two Latin words that echo the title of the constitution, though in reverse order (*Verbum Dei*, "Word of God").

Paragraph 17

> The word of God, which to everyone who has faith contains God's
> saving power (see Rom 1:16), is set forth and marvelously displays its
> power in the writings of the New Testament. For when the time had
> fully come (see Gal 4:4), the Word became flesh and dwelt among us,
> full of grace and truth (see Jn 1:14). Christ established on earth the
> kingdom of God, revealed his Father and himself by deeds and words,
> and by his death, resurrection and glorious ascension, as well as by
> sending the Holy Spirit, completed his work. Lifted up from the earth
> he draws all people to himself (Jn 12:32, Greek text), for he alone has the
> words of eternal life (see Jn 6:68). This mystery was not made known
> to other generations as it has now been revealed to his holy apostles
> and prophets by the Holy Spirit (see Eph 3:4-6, Greek text), that they
> might preach the Gospel, foster faith in Jesus, Christ and Lord, and
> bring together the church. The writings of the New Testament stand
> as a perpetual and divine witness to these realities.

The first numbered paragraph (17) in this chapter orients the discussion of the New Testament by showing that this is where the "mystery"
of God's great plan of salvation for all humankind gets revealed and
preserved. It mentions explicitly "when the time had fully come," a New
Testament expression (such as in Gal 4:4) that explains God's definitive
revelation in terms of the incarnation, the coming of Christ as the Word
made flesh (as in John 1:14). Through his life, death, resurrection, and
ascension and then the sending of the Holy Spirit upon his apostles,
Christ fulfilled all the hopes of the Old Testament prophets and brought
the eternal truth of salvation to be spread by the apostles. Twice the
paragraph mentions the Holy Spirit, emphasizing the Spirit's role in
empowering the evangelical mission of the apostles, and in guiding the
preaching and establishment of the church.

The entire paragraph moves toward its climax in the proclamation
of the permanent value of the books of the New Testament: they "stand
as a perpetual and divine witness to these realities." In fact, one notes
in this paragraph a very Christ-centered (Christocentric*) focus. For instance, the "deeds and words" of Christ are mentioned again, as well as
his passion and resurrection. This Christocentrism indeed is one of the
characteristics of *Dei Verbum* that sets it apart from the dogmatic teaching
of Vatican Council I, which was much more God-centered (theocentric)
in its teaching. Here the constitution underlines the importance of the
New Testament as bringing God's message of salvation to full fruition

through Jesus Christ the Lord. Yet we note, too, that the paragraph does not lose sight of the pneumatological emphasis found in *Dei Verbum*, for the Holy Spirit is also referenced even here.

An easily overlooked point in this paragraph is the double reference to the *Greek* text of the New Testament with regard to two passages (John 12:32; Eph 3:4-6; also elsewhere in DV, 10 and 11). This is a subtle reminder of the original language of the New Testament (*Koinē* Greek, not Latin) and the fact that the Latin Vulgate text sometimes is not sufficient to get at the literal meaning of the biblical text.

The next numbered paragraph (18) then turns its attention to the four canonical gospels and why they are so honored in the Christian tradition.

Paragraph 18

> It is common knowledge that among all the inspired writings, including those of the New Testament, the Gospels have a special place, and rightly so, because they are our principal source for the life and teaching of the incarnate Word, our Savior.
>
> The church has always and everywhere maintained, and continues to maintain, the apostolic origin of the four Gospels. The apostles preached, as Christ had charged them to do, and then, under the inspiration of the Holy Spirit, they and others of the apostolic age handed on to us in writing the same message they had preached, the foundation of our faith: the fourfold Gospel, according to Matthew, Mark, Luke and John.[31]

With the splendor of the New Testament set forth, the constitution narrows its focus somewhat in paragraph 18 by underlining the privileged place accorded the four canonical gospels—Matthew, Mark, Luke, John—in church tradition. We see this special honor visibly displayed in the church's practice of standing for the proclamation of the gospel at Mass, the use of a "book of the gospels" for certain liturgical ceremonies, and the periodic enthronement of the latter in a prominent place in church. *Dei Verbum* explains the reason for honoring the gospels simply: "because they are our principal source for the life and teaching of the incarnate Word, our Savior."

This paragraph makes two other important assertions about the gospels. First, they have always been reverenced because of their *apostolic* origin. That is, they came from the preaching of the apostles in accordance with the command they had received from the Lord Jesus himself. Second, the gospels, like all the Sacred Scriptures, were handed on under "the inspiration of the Holy Spirit." The original Latin text (*Divino afflante Spiritu*) here is interesting because it alludes literally to the title of the 1943 encyclical letter of Pope Pius XII that helped influence the formulation of the constitution and that also gave impetus to the modern, critical study of the Bible by Catholic scholars. (See chapter 3 of this book below where this is explained further.) As in chapters 1 and 2 of the constitution, the Holy Spirit is the guarantor of the authenticity and truth of the Scriptures. That is why the church reverences them as divinely authored books.

Narrowing its focus even further, the next numbered paragraph (19) goes on to address the thorny question of the historical reliability of the gospels.

Paragraph 19

> Holy mother church has firmly and with absolute constancy maintained and continues to maintain, that these four Gospels, whose historicity it unhesitatingly affirms, faithfully hand on what Jesus, the Son of God, while he lived among men and women, really did and taught for their eternal salvation, until the day when he was taken up (see Acts 1:1-2). For, after the ascension of the Lord, the apostles handed on to their hearers what he had said and done, but with that fuller understanding which they, instructed by the glorious events of Christ and enlightened by the Spirit of truth,[32] now enjoyed.[33] The sacred authors, in writing the four Gospels, selected certain of the many elements which had been handed on, either orally or in written form; others they synthesized or explained with an eye to the situation of the churches. They retained the preaching style, but always in such a fashion that they have told us the authentic truth about Jesus.[34] Whether they relied on their own memory and recollections or on the testimony of those who "from the beginning were eyewitnesses and ministers of the word," their purpose in writing was that we might know the "truth" concerning the things of which we have been informed (see Lk 1:2-4).

This paragraph (19) addresses one of the most delicate issues tackled by *Dei Verbum*, namely, the historical truth of the gospels. The very first Latin words of this paragraph (*Sancta mater ecclesia*) directly recall the title of a document of the Pontifical Biblical Commission, promulgated in April 1964, more than a year before the final approval of *Dei Verbum*. At the time, we should recall that the Biblical Commission was a teaching arm of the Congregation for the Doctrine of the Faith, although Pope Paul VI's reforms of the Roman Curia (Vatican offices) in 1971 relegated it to an advisory body of that same Congregation. The important point is that this entire paragraph (19) has been stamped with the teaching of this famous document of the Biblical Commission.

At the heart of the teaching of paragraph 19 is the understanding of the long and complex process the gospels underwent as they were being formulated. The paragraph fully adopts the explanation of *Sancta Mater Ecclesia*, which affirmed that three levels of ancient tradition are embedded in the gospels:

(1) the level of Jesus' own teaching;

(2) the level of the apostles' preaching and oral proclamation;

(3) the level of the collecting, sorting, editing, organizing the oral traditions about Jesus.

What does this teaching mean? It is distinctly not an attack on the historicity of the gospels. The paragraph clearly states three times (beginning, middle, and end) in different words that the gospels are reliable in terms of history. They preserve the "truth" (Latin, *veritatem*) about Jesus of Nazareth, his ministry, death, resurrection, and ascension. Yet the acknowledgment of the process whereby the traditions about Jesus were proclaimed and passed on from generation to generation, and that at least three levels of "history" must be recognized in the gospels, indicates that one cannot naively assume the *literal* historical details of each and every gospel story. The paragraph explicitly states that the evangelists "selected" their materials, "synthesized," and "explained" them with an eye to their own contexts. By quoting Luke 1:2-4 the document also acknowledges that there were different levels of "tradition" that lay behind the formulation of the gospels. Luke, the most historically conscious of the evangelists, spoke of relying on "eyewitnesses and ministers of the word," subtly implying that he himself was not one of them. Yet he set out to put the story of Jesus in an orderly fashion so that the "truth" of it could be preserved for his community and for all ages (cf. also Acts 1:1-5).

This paragraph, then, shows the influence of biblical and theological experts who, behind the scenes, helped the framers of the constitution to arrive at a nuanced explanation of some complex questions, like the historicity of the gospels. Although the fathers of the council, the bishops, had to vote on and approve the final texts of all the council documents, this paragraph shows how they also relied on the expertise of others at times to help the final formulation.

The next and final numbered paragraph (20) of the chapter wraps up the discussion of the New Testament by mentioning in brief fashion other writings beyond the gospels.

Paragraph 20

> Besides the four Gospels, the New Testament also contains the letters of St. Paul and other apostolic writings composed under the inspiration of the Holy Spirit. In accordance with God's wise design these writings firmly establish those matters which concern Christ the Lord, formulate more precisely his authentic teaching, preach the saving power of Christ's divine work and foretell its glorious consummation.
>
> For the Lord Jesus was with his apostles as he had promised (see Mt 28:20) and he had sent to them the Spirit, the Counselor, who would guide them into all truth (see Jn 16:13).

Having highlighted the preeminence of the gospels, the chapter concludes with its final paragraph (20) on the other canonical New Testament writings, mentioning the epistles of Saint Paul explicitly. Paul's name, after all, is found on thirteen of the twenty-seven books of the New Testament. Moreover, he is cited some thirty-two times in *Dei Verbum*, indicating his importance as a biblical resource for the church's teaching on revelation. The paragraph concludes this chapter by reiterating that all the New Testament writings were composed under the Holy Spirit's guidance and therefore contain reliable and authentic teaching about Jesus Christ and the significance of his saving power.

Chapter VI: Sacred Scripture in the Life of the Church (pars. 21–26)

The final chapter of *Dei Verbum* gets at what some might consider "the payoff" of the church's teaching—the "so what?" question. What role does Sacred Scripture play for Catholics in the life of the church? The final six numbered paragraphs of the dogmatic constitution address the pastoral implications of its doctrinal teachings. (Indeed, we should emphasize that there is no conflict between the notions of pastoral and doctrinal interpretation of Vatican II, as if the two could be entirely separated.)

Paragraph 21

> The church has always venerated the divine scriptures as it has venerated the Body of the Lord, in that it never ceases, above all in the sacred liturgy, to partake of the bread of life and offer it to the faithful from the one table of the word of God and the Body of Christ. It has always regarded and continues to regard the scriptures, taken together with sacred tradition, as the supreme rule of its faith. For, since they are inspired by God and committed to writing once and for all time, they present God's own word in an unalterable form, and they make the voice of the Holy Spirit sound again and again in the words of the prophets and apostles. It follows that all the preaching of the church, as indeed the entire Christian religion, should be nourished and ruled by sacred scripture. In the sacred books the Father who is in heaven comes lovingly to meet his children, and talks with them. And such is the force and power of the word of God that it is the church's support and strength, imparting robustness to the faith of its daughters and sons and providing food for their souls. It is a pure and unfailing fount of spiritual life. It is eminently true of holy scripture that: "the word of God is living and active" (Heb 4:12), and "is able to build you up and give you the inheritance among all those who are sanctified" (Acts 20:32; see 1 Th 2:13).

The first numbered paragraph (21) of the chapter begins with what can only be considered a most remarkable statement for Catholics to make: "The church has always venerated the divine scriptures as it has venerated the Body of the Lord . . ." This is an assertion of the equal veneration of Word and sacrament, of the Sacred Scriptures and the Eucharist. Lest the import of this statement be overlooked, the paragraph explains this sacramental insight by speaking of the church offering the faithful the bread of life "from the one table of the word of God and the Body of Christ." Essentially, this means that the proclamation of the Sacred Scriptures communicates "bread of life" just as the reception of the Eucharist does.

This assertion is not far from the teaching in *Lumen Gentium*, the Dogmatic Constitution on the Church adopted by the council in 1963, that there are multiple ways in which the risen Lord is present in the church, including in the proclamation of the Word at liturgy (LG 7).

Unfortunately, over time prior to Vatican II, Catholics focused only on the "real presence" in the Eucharist and forgot the real presence of the Lord in the Word. What Vatican II restored was the balance between Word and sacrament. This was not an entirely novel teaching of the council. Its roots go back at least to Saint Augustine, who is cited in the seventeenth century by a great spiritual writer, Jean-Jacques Olier (1608–57), founder of my own community of diocesan priests (Sulpicians). He uses a quotation from Saint Augustine to exhort his followers to respect both Word and sacrament:

> God has two treasures for which he made the church his depository: the first is his body and precious blood; the second is the Word or his Scripture and divine testament, which is the deposit of his secrets and divine wishes . . . Now this holy treasure of the Sacred Scriptures has been given into the hands of his bride the Church by the goodness of God. . . . We should treat it [the Word of God] with even more respect because one must have more faith to respect it and give it the reverence it merits, following Saint Augustine's remarks when he says that he wants us to give the same respect to the least syllables of Scripture that we give to the particles of the Blessed Sacrament, because they are like envelopes, curtains and sacraments which contain the Holy Spirit, being the ordinary but entirely divine instrument through which he acts in the church. (*Traité des Saints Ordres* [Sulpician Archives, Paris], 125–26, author's translation; cf. Saint Augustine, Sermon 300.2)

Dei Verbum proceeds to pair together two other concepts that too often are seen as opposites, Scripture and tradition. Again, a rather startling statement is made: the church "has always regarded and continues to regard the scriptures, taken together with sacred tradition, as the supreme rule of its faith." This harks back to the earlier teaching of *Dei Verbum* (pars. 9–10) that Scripture and tradition are not two separate sources of revelation but one unified way in which God reveals himself to the faithful and to the world. The constitution employs a beautiful, personalistic image to describe this process of God's self-revelation: "In the sacred books, the Father who is in heaven comes lovingly to meet his children, and talks with them." This is truly a personal and dialogical view of revelation. God acts like a father concerned for his children. The Scriptures, under the guidance of the Holy Spirit, are God's word to the people. They bring the church support and give it energy; they nourish, strengthen, and feed God's people. They are explicitly called "food for their souls," and by means of several biblical quotations the word of God is acknowledged as "living and active" (Heb 4:12), with the capability to "build up" the faithful (Acts 20:32; also 1 Thess 2:13).

This opening paragraph, then, boldly asserts the perpetual value of the Scriptures as God's word. They nourish and sustain the faithful as does the Eucharist itself, the prime sacrament of Catholic identity and spiritual nourishment for all the faithful, which *Lumen Gentium* calls "the source and summit of the Christian life" (LG 11). The paragraph also asserts that all preaching in the church should be based on Sacred Scripture, a reminder to the clergy to make their homilies more biblically based. This powerful and dynamic presentation sets up the application of the Scriptures on several more practical levels, which the subsequent paragraphs address.

Paragraph 22

> Access to sacred scripture ought to be widely available to the Christian faithful. For this reason the church, from the very beginning, made its own the ancient translation of the Old Testament called the Septuagint; it honors also the other eastern translations, and the Latin translations, especially that known as the Vulgate. But since the word of God must be readily available at all times, the church, with motherly concern, sees to it that suitable and correct translations are made into various languages, especially from the original texts of the sacred books. If, when the opportunity presents itself and the authorities of the church agree, these translations are made jointly with churches separated from us, they can then be used by all Christians.

Given the importance of Sacred Scripture for the church, the next numbered paragraph (22) specifically makes some recommendations that go beyond the boundaries of the Catholic Church. First is the statement that the Scriptures should become more accessible to all the Christian faithful. The "ecumenical" nature of the council—here understood as interdenominational dialogue—shines forth as an implication that can affect all Christians. This position is all the more impressive when one recalls that in 1711 Pope Clement XI had condemned the notion that the Scriptures should be accessible to everyone as too "Protestant"! The prime example the constitution invokes as evidence that the church desires this broad accessibility to Scripture is the Septuagint,* the Greek translation of the Old Testament (Hebrew Bible), which was undertaken to preserve the Jewish scriptural traditions when the Jews were in danger of losing their native language in the Diaspora* (the Jewish dispersion to regions apart from the Holy Land after the first destruction of Jerusalem in 587 BC).

A second example of this pastoral desire to spread the word of God is the Latin Vulgate. Saint Jerome (ca. AD 340–420) undertook this translation from the original languages (Hebrew and Greek), based on earlier Latin manuscripts, to make the Word accessible in the Latin-speaking world of his day. The paragraph takes a further step to promote accessibility. Jumping to modern times, it says that the church, "with motherly concern" (a tender parental image), wants to make the Scriptures even more available by fostering translations into many modern languages. In addition, the document calls for joint ecumenical translations wherever possible, if other denominations would agree to such an enterprise. This in fact became a reality, but at the time *Dei Verbum* was being formulated, such a stunning development of ecumenical translations was almost unthinkable after some four hundred years of post-Reformation divisive rhetoric among Christians. Nonetheless *Dei Verbum* is testimony to the Catholic Church's admirable goal of helping "all Christians" have access to the word of God precisely because it offers the words of salvation for the whole world.

With the next numbered paragraph (23), the pastoral tone and direction of the constitution continues.

Paragraph 23

> Taught by the Holy Spirit, the spouse of the incarnate Word, which is the church, strives to reach an increasingly more profound understanding of the sacred scriptures, in order to nourish its children with God's words. For this reason also it duly encourages the study of the Fathers, both eastern and western, and of the sacred liturgies. Catholic exegetes and other workers in the field of sacred theology should work diligently together and under the watchful eye of the sacred magisterium. Using appropriate techniques they should together set about examining and explaining the sacred texts in such a way that as many as possible of those who are ministers of God's word may be able to dispense fruitfully the nourishment of the scriptures to the people of God. This nourishment enlightens the mind, strengthens the will and fires the hearts of men and women with the love of God.[35] The holy synod encourages those members of the church who are engaged

in biblical studies constantly to renew their efforts, in order to carry on, with complete dedication and in accordance with the mind of the church, the work they have so happily begun.[36]

This next paragraph (23) returns to other aspects of *Dei Verbum*'s promotion of a pastoral use of the Word. Using the evocative image of the church as "the spouse of the incarnate Word," that is, the church as the bride of Christ, the paragraph expresses the desire of the church to feed her "children [literally, sons] with God's words." This is another maternal image. The council fathers viewed the church as a concerned and loving "mother" who wants only the best for her sons and daughters. But there is also recognition that the church does not accomplish this mission of nourishment without help. To this end, the paragraph mentions several important resources for its task of disseminating the word of God:

- the fathers of the church, both East and West, who often made commentaries on the Scriptures and preached on them with eloquence;
- Catholic exegetes and theologians, that is, professional scholars who study the Bible in the original languages and help deepen biblical interpretation;
- the church's liturgical rites, where the word of God has always prominently been a feature and which actually influenced the shape of some of the Scriptures;
- various "ministers of God's word" who are charged with disseminating the word of God to nourish people, to enlighten them intellectually, and to set their "hearts on fire" with the Word.

These words of encouragement are especially directed to Catholic biblical scholars who are encouraged to do their work diligently and cooperatively with one another. They are also expressly asked to do their research in union with the mind of the church. This is no "free license" to engage in personal fanciful biblical interpretation or to embrace every passing fad of biblical interpretation. Rather, Catholic exegetes are urged to do their research responsibly "under the watchful eye of the sacred magisterium" and "in accordance with the mind of the church."

The next paragraph (24) then turns to a broad appreciation of the importance of the word of God, continuing in the vein of the function of the Scriptures in pastoral practice.

Paragraph 24

> Sacred theology relies on the written word of God, taken together with sacred tradition, as its permanent foundation. By this word it is powerfully strengthened and constantly rejuvenated, as it searches out, under the light of the faith, all the truth stored up in the mystery of Christ. The sacred scriptures contain the word of God, and, because they are inspired, they truly are the word of God; therefore, the study of the sacred page should be the very soul of sacred theology.[37] The ministry of the word, too—pastoral preaching, catechetics and all forms of Christian instruction, among which the liturgical homily should hold pride of place—gains healthy nourishment and holy vitality from the word of scripture.

In emphasizing the broad applicability of the Scriptures to ecclesial life, this paragraph (24) provides one of the document's most memorable and oft-quoted lines: "the study of the sacred page should be the very soul of sacred theology." What a profound image! Nothing touches the inmost being of theology more than pouring over the Scriptures. They function like the "very soul" of theological reflection. The paragraph reiterates the truth that theology has always relied upon the written word of God and tradition, both of which together provide a "permanent foundation." The two concepts are united again as one source to help express the "truth" (singular) of revelation. In this context, the document then names the key pastoral ministries of the Word that help to bring about its authentic interpretation: pastoral preachers, catechists, and diverse Christian teachings. Among them, pride of place is given to the "liturgical homily," thus implying the importance of preachers of the word of God at liturgy (that is, bishops, priests, or deacons, those in ordained ministry). This observation leads directly to the next paragraph, where the ordained, who are most entrusted with responsibility for preaching the Word, are instructed explicitly.

The next numbered paragraph (25) of the constitution turns its attention to various individuals in the church who are important resources for disseminating the teaching of the Sacred Scriptures.

Paragraph 25

> Therefore, all clerics, particularly priests of Christ and others who, as deacons or catechists, are officially engaged in the ministry of the word, should immerse themselves in the scriptures by constant spiritual read-

ing and diligent study. For it must not happen that any of them become "empty preachers of the word of God to others, not being hearers of the word in their own hearts,"[38] when they ought to be sharing the boundless riches of the divine word with the faithful committed to their care, especially in the sacred liturgy. Likewise, the holy synod forcefully and specifically exhorts all the Christian faithful, especially those who live the religious life, to learn "the surpassing knowledge of Jesus Christ" (Phil 3:8) by frequent reading of the sacred scriptures. "Ignorance of Scripture is ignorance of Christ."[39] Therefore, let them go gladly to the sacred text itself, whether in the sacred liturgy, which is full of the divine words, or in devout reading, or in such suitable exercises and in various other helps which, with the approval and guidance of the pastors of the church, are happily spreading everywhere in our day. Let them remember, however, that prayer should accompany the reading of sacred scripture, so that it becomes a dialogue between God and the human reader. For, "we speak to him when we pray; we listen to him when we read the divine oracles."[40]

It is the duty of bishops, "with whom the apostolic doctrine resides,"[41] suitably to instruct the faithful entrusted to them in the correct use of the divine books, especially the New Testament and in particular the Gospels. This is done by translations of the sacred texts which are equipped with necessary and really adequate explanations. Thus, the children of the church can familiarize themselves safely and profitably with the sacred scriptures, and become steeped in their spirit.

Moreover, editions of sacred scripture, provided with suitable notes, should be prepared for the use even of non-Christians, and adapted to their circumstances. These should be prudently circulated, either by pastors of souls or by Christians of any walk of life.

This numbered paragraph (25), with its several sections, addresses almost all levels of membership in the church with regard to the task of getting more familiar with the word of God by frequent reading, studying, and praying the Scriptures. Anyone officially engaged in the ministry of the Word is encouraged in this regard—priests, deacons, catechists, in particular. Two patristic quotations are used to exhort such ministers to be worthy of their special task. Saint Augustine's words remind us of the importance of first "hearing" the word of God so that we may better proclaim it. This point became a vital issue for the "new evangelization" project fostered by Saint John Paul II and Pope Benedict XVI, emphasizing the need for church members to hear the word and take it to heart in order to more effectively give it to others.

For his part, Saint Jerome is favorably quoted for his well-known statement, "Ignorance of the scriptures is ignorance of Christ." Jerome never minces words. He gets to the heart of the matter. Reading Scripture puts us in touch with Jesus Christ. The risen Lord is indeed present in the Word. Thus, the paragraph exhorts all the faithful, and especially those in religious life, to become more familiar with Scripture, whether through the liturgy or frequent devout reading. Then the image of dialogue returns that was prominent in the first paragraphs of *Dei Verbum*. The Scriptures facilitate this dialogue with God; they are an essential element of divine revelation.

The final section of this paragraph turns its attention to the particular responsibilities of bishops, who notably have been absent in the earlier advice. Because of their unique role as successors to the apostles, bishops bear special responsibility for promoting appreciation of the word of God. They are special stewards of the Word. They are urged to provide the faithful with good, authentic translations that can help people understand the sacred words better. In particular, special study Bibles with notes and explanatory comments are encouraged, to be distributed widely and accessible to all Christians. This desire clearly expresses the pastoral goal of the council to ensure that the gift of God's revelation is widely distributed and made accessible to all. In essence, this is a call for good quality resources for Bible study.

Finally approaching its conclusion in the final paragraph (26), the constitution ends on a hope-filled note inspired by the Scriptures themselves.

Paragraph 26

> So may it come that, by the reading and study of the sacred books "the word of God may speed on and triumph" (2 Th 3:1) and the treasure of revelation entrusted to the church may more and more fill people's hearts. Just as from constant attendance at the eucharistic mystery the life of the church draws increase, so a new impulse of spiritual life may be expected from increased veneration of the word of God, which "stands forever" (Is 40:8; see 1 Pet 1:23-25).

The final paragraph (26) of *Dei Verbum* concludes on a hopeful note of exhortation, quoting a wish from Saint Paul that "'the word of God may speed on and triumph' (2 Th 3:1)." It also calls Scripture the sacred "treasure of revelation" that has been entrusted to the church and that hopefully will impact the lives of all people. Then, reiterating the relationship the constitution had spoken of earlier, the paragraph expresses the wish that reverence of the word of God will impact the life of the church just as frequent eucharistic celebration strengthens her. The careful balance of Word and sacrament is thus maintained to the conclusion of the constitution, which finally asserts confidently that the word of God will "stand forever," citing passages from both the Old and New Testaments (Isa 40:8; 1 Pet 1:23-25).

General Assessment of *Dei Verbum*

The commentary above is obviously modest in its explanation of the riches of this dogmatic constitution. One cannot overestimate its importance in the life of the church in the twenty-first century. It tackled important and controverted questions like the relationship between Scripture, tradition and the magisterium, inspiration, inerrancy, and the pastoral application of the Scriptures to church life. If the last fifty years of history have provided many opportunities to deepen our appreciation of this remarkable document, the next fifty will doubtless enable us to comprehend in even greater depth how this ecumenical teaching helped the church to rediscover the power of the word of God in modern times.

This overview allows us an opportunity to draw attention to some of the primary features of *Dei Verbum*. Although it proclaimed no new dogmas or doctrines, it deepened considerably the church's understanding of revelation and of Sacred Scripture. It was also the first time the church had in an official teaching explored the relationship between Scripture and tradition in any depth. There can also be no doubt that the Catholic rediscovery of the power of the Scriptures helped to rejuvenate the church for subsequent decades.

At the risk of reducing the teaching of *Dei Verbum* too much, I offer here a brief list of fifteen key teachings of this dogmatic constitution that continue to impact the church's life:

- Revelation is the gracious, loving, personal outreach of God toward sinful humanity, offering fellowship and salvation.
- Revelation is also part of the mystery of God and as such can never be fully comprehended by the human mind until we meet God face-to-face; revelation inherently has theological, christological, pneumatological, and trinitarian dimensions.

- God is the ultimate source and goal of revelation; God's revelation is seen in both the words and deeds God has accomplished through the history of salvation.

- Jesus Christ is both the ultimate mediator and the sum total of revelation; Christ is the one in whom we encounter the invisible God made visible through his Son.

- Revelation is mediated through the incarnation, both in terms of the Word made flesh and in terms of the word of God expressed in human terms.

- The Old Testament prepared for and finds its fulfillment in the New Testament, and the New Testament sheds light on and helps explain the Old Testament; both are fully the word of God.

- No new revelation can be expected but human comprehension of revelation is continually deepened over the ages.

- The Holy Spirit, who figures prominently throughout *Dei Verbum*, is the guarantor of both the inspiration of Sacred Scripture and the faithful tradition of the church handed on from the apostles.

- The doctrine of the inspiration of Scripture is affirmed but no exact theory of how it operates is adopted; the Scriptures are without error with regard to the necessary teaching for salvation.

- Tradition and Scripture constitute one source of divine revelation, and they are intimately intertwined.

- The magisterium of the church has the definitive authority to interpret the Scriptures where needed, but it also remains the servant of the Word and not its master; the exact relationship between Scripture, tradition, and magisterium is left open-ended, but they are intimately interrelated.

- The Catholic Church embraces an ecumenical approach to Scripture translation and study.

- Catholic exegesis or interpretation of Scripture should be exercised in the broader context of the living tradition of the church, the unity of the Scriptures, and the analogy of faith.

- Because they are divinely inspired, the Scriptures provide a reliable guide for teaching, moral instruction, prayer, liturgy, and meditation.

• Catholic exegetes should pay careful attention to literary forms, styles of writing, and cultural influences when interpreting the Scriptures, and do their work in union with and under the guidance of the magisterium.

Notes to the text of *Dei Verbum*

1. St. Augustine, *De Catechizandis rudibus*, 4, 8: PL 40, 316.

2. See Mt 11:27; Jn 1:14 and 17; 14:6; 17:1-3; 2 Cor 3:16 and 4:6; Eph 1:3-14.

3. *Letter to Diognetus*, 7, 4: Funk, *Patres Apostolici*, I, p. 403.

4. Vatican Council I, Dogmatic Constitution on the Catholic Faith, *Dei Filius*, ch. 3: Denz. 1789 (3008).

5. Council of Orange II, canon 7: Denz. 180 (377). Vatican Council I, loc. cit.: Denz. 1791 (3010).

6. Vatican Council I, Dogmatic Constitution on the Catholic Faith, *Dei Filius*, ch. 2: Denz. 1786 (3005).

7. Ibid.: Denz. 1785 and 1786 (3004 and 3005).

8. See Mt 28:19-20 and Mk 16:15. Council of Trent, Decree *On the Canonical Scriptures*: Denz. 783 (1501).

9. See Council of Trent, loc. cit.; Vatican Council I, Dogmatic Constitution on the Catholic Faith, *Dei Filius*, ch. 2: Denz. 1787 (3006).

10. St. Irenaeus, *Adv. Haer.*, III, 3,1: PG 7, 848; Harvey, 2, p. 9.

11. See Council of Nicea II: Denz. 303 (602). Council of Constantinople IV, Session X, can. 1: Denz. 336 (650–652).

12. See Vatican Council I, Dogmatic Constitution on the Catholic Faith, *Dei Filius*, ch. 4: Denz. 1800 (3020).

13. See Council of Trent, Decree *On the Canonical Scriptures*: Denz. 783 (1501).

14. See Pius XII, Apost. Const. *Munificentissimus Deus*, 1 Nov. 1950: AAS 42 (1950), p. 756, taken along with the words of St. Cyprian, *Epist.* 66, 8: CSEL, III, 2, 733: "The church is the people united to its priests, the flock adhering to its shepherd."

15. See Vatican Council I, Dogmatic Constitution on the Catholic Faith, *Dei Filius*, ch. 3: Denz. 1972 (3011).

16. See Pius XII, Encyclical *Humani Generis*, 12 Aug. 1950: AAS 42 (1950) 568–569: Denz. 2314 (3886).

17. See Vatican Council I, Dogmatic Constitution on the Catholic Faith, *Dei Filius*, ch. 2: Denz. 1787 (3006). Pontifical Biblical Commission, Decree 18 June 1915: Denz. 2180 (3629); EB 420. Holy Office, *Letter*, 22 Dec. 1923: EB 499.

18. See Pius XII, Encyclical *Divino Afflante Spiritu*, 30 Sept. 1943: AAS 35 (1943), p. 314; EB 556.

19. *In* and *through* human beings: see Heb 1:1 and 4:7 (*in*); 2 Kg 23:2; Mt 1:22 and *passim* (through); Vatican Council I, Schema on Catholic doctrine, note 9: Collectio Lacensis, VII, 522.

20. Leo XIII, Encyclical *Providentissimus Deus*, 18 Nov. 1893: Denz. 1952 (3293); EB 125.

21. See St. Augustine, *De Gen. ad Litt.*, 2, 9, 20: PL 34, 270–271; *Epistola 82*, 3: PL 33, 277; CSEL 34, 2, p. 354. St. Thomas Aquinas, *De Veritate*, q. 12, a 2, C. Council of Trent, Session IV, On the canonical scriptures: Denz. 783 (1501); Leo XIII, Encyclical *Providentissimus Deus*: EB 121, 124, 126–127. Pius XII, Encyclical *Divino Afflante Spiritu*: EB 539.

22. St. Augustine, *De Civitate Dei*, XVII, 6, 2: PL 41, 537; CSEL 40, 2, 228.

23. St. Augustine, *De Doctrina Christiana*, III, 18, 26: PL 34, 75–76.

24. Pius XII, loc. cit.: Denz. 2294 (3829–3830); EB 557–562.

25. See Benedict XV, Encyclical *Spiritus Paraclitus*, 15 Sept. 1920; EB 469. St. Jerome, *In Gal.* 5, 19–21: PL 26, 417 A.

26. See Vatican Council I, Dogmatic Constitution on the Catholic Faith, *Dei Filius*, ch. 2: Denz. 1788 (3007).

27. St. John Chrysostom, *In Gen.* 3, 8 (homily 17, 1): PG 53, 134. *Attemperatio* corresponds to the Greek *synkatabasis*.

28. Pius XI, *Mit brennender Sorge*, 14 March 1937: AAS 29 (1937), p. 151.

29. St. Augustine, *Quaest. in Hept.* 2, 73: PL 34, 623.

30. St. Irenaeus, *Adv. Haer.*, III, 21, 3: PG 7, 950 (= 25, 1: Harvey 2, p. 115). St. Cyril of Jerusalem, *Catech.* 4, 35: PG 33, 497. Theodore of Mopsuestia, *In Soph.* 1, 4–6: PG 66, 452D–453A.

31. See St. Irenaeus, *Adv. Haer.*, III, 11, 8: PG 7, 885; ed. Sagnard, p. 194.

32. See Jn 14:26; 16:13.

33. Jn 2:22; 12:16; see 14:26; 16:12-13; 7:39.

34. See the Instruction *Sancta Mater Ecclesia* of the Pontifical Biblical Commission: AAS 56 (1964), p. 715.

35. See Pius XII, Encyclical *Divino Afflante*: EB 551, 553, 567. Pontifical Biblical Commission, *Instructio de S. Scriptura in Clericorum Seminariis et Religiosorum Collegiis recte docenda*, 13 May 1950: AAS 42 (1950), pp. 495–505.

36. See Pius XII, ibid.: EB 569.

37. See Leo XIII, Encyclical *Providentissimus Deus*: EB 114; Benedict XV, Encyclical *Spiritus Paraclitus*: EB 483.

38. St. Augustine, *Serm.* 179: PL 38, 966.

39. St. Jerome, *Comm. in Isaias*, Prol.: PL 24, 17. See Benedict XV, Encyclical *Spiritus Paraclitus*: EB 475–480; Pius XII, Encyclical *Divino Afflante*: EB 544.

40. St. Ambrose, *De Officiis ministrorum* I, 20, 88: PL 16, 50.

41. St. Irenaeus, *Adv. Haer.*, IV, 32, 1: PG 7, 1071 (= 49, 2) Harvey, 2, p. 255.

CHAPTER THREE

Ongoing Interpretation and the Fruits of *Dei Verbum*

The fifty years since the promulgation of *Dei Verbum* have seen incredible developments among Catholics of knowledge and appreciation of Sacred Scripture. The Bible has become much more prominent in the life of the church and in the lives of the average Catholic. Yet this has not been without controversy, nor has this led universally to the same appreciation of the impact of *Dei Verbum* on Catholic life. Many controversies have erupted over the interpretation of several documents of the council, perhaps none sharper than those surrounding *Dei Verbum*. In this chapter we will take a closer look at some of these controversies and what is at stake fifty years after the end of the council. We will also consider some "fruits" of this landmark document.

The Implementation of *Dei Verbum*

Although it was one of the last documents of the council to be approved and promulgated, *Dei Verbum* was one that began to have virtually an immediate impact on Catholic life. One reason for this was that Catholic biblical scholars had been quietly doing their work for decades prior to the council, so they were immediately prepared to begin fostering among Catholics an appreciation of the Bible once the constitution was issued. Little Rock Scripture Study, which began in the Diocese of Little Rock (Arkansas) in 1974, is one example of the kind of high-quality Bible study programs that began to make inroads among Catholics in order to promote better understanding of the Sacred Scriptures. It implemented well the vision of *Dei Verbum* regarding the promotion of Bible study (DV 25). Catholics, it was discovered, were thirsty for the word of God. They were largely interested to know more about the Bible and its teachings. There was, then, a built-in audience of at least some Catholics whose desire for more knowledge of the Bible would lead them to become engaged in such formal programs.

Another fruit of *Dei Verbum* was the promotion of ecumenical discussions. Of course, the Secretariat for Promoting Christian Unity had itself been instrumental in helping design *Dei Verbum*. But the constitution truly brought a breath of fresh air to ecumenism that had already begun with the Decree on Ecumenism, *Unitatis Redintegratio* ("The Restoration of Unity"), issued on November 21, 1964. After centuries of Protestant and Catholic division because of a difference of understanding about Scripture and tradition, *Dei Verbum* gave the green light for Catholics to appreciate the Bible in all its splendor and to dialogue with Protestants. This new openness allowed for official dialogues with Anglicans, Lutherans, Methodists, Evangelicals, and others, which resulted at times in helpful studies or church statements that fostered better mutual understanding.

Also, Vatican II's other reforms, such as those connected to the liturgy and priestly formation, allowed for broader access to the Bible and stressed its importance for preaching and moral instruction. The Scriptures became more integrated into daily Catholic life. The revised Lectionary* gave access to many more biblical readings than before, and seminaries offered more courses on Scripture and homiletics and tried to promote better biblical preaching among the clergy.

In short, *Dei Verbum* remains one of the great successes of Vatican II in the sense that its impact was widespread and is still ongoing. Fortunately, the fiftieth anniversary of the constitution has also given a push to go back to the "well" of this profound document so that we can once again drink of its refreshing teaching.

An element of the debate about the Second Vatican Council that continues to this day is the question of which document is the most important. *Dei Verbum* figures significantly in this debate. There is no doubt that the four constitutions outrank in authority the other documents of the council (decrees and declarations), but two of these are given the further description of "dogmatic" constitutions, *Dei Verbum* and *Lumen Gentium* ("Light to the Nations"), the Dogmatic Constitution on the Church issued on November 21, 1964, a year before *Dei Verbum*.

Both are clearly the highest level teachings of the council, and both treat essential matters: revelation and the nature of the church (ecclesiology*). To muddy the waters further, some scholars propose that the most important document of the council is *Sacrosanctum Concilium* ("The Sacred Council"), the Constitution on the Sacred Liturgy issued on December 4, 1963, nearly two years prior to *Dei Verbum*. Their argument is that the tremendous reforms made in the liturgy made a greater impact on the practical lives of Catholics and gave direction for the rest of the council's work. At stake is which document may have provided the most influence within the council itself and thus provides the most important optic through which to view the final results of the council.

The debate is likely to go on for some time, and there are pros and cons on the various sides of the argument. But we should also note that the Doctrinal Commission of Vatican II, which played a major role in preparing the draft documents, underlined the primary importance of *Dei Verbum* by stating that it was "in a way the first of all the constitutions of this council, so that its Preface introduces them all to a certain extent" (cited in O. Rush, "Toward a Comprehensive Interpretation of the Council and Its Documents," *Theological Studies* 73:3 [2012]: 568). For our purposes, we can simply note that, though *Dei Verbum* was a late "child" of the council, its teaching is wide-ranging and foundational to the church's own self-understanding. An extraordinary synod of bishops held in 1985 to examine the achievements of Vatican II and promote its authentic interpretation noted that *Dei Verbum* was a "neglected" document from the council whose basic teaching of the necessity of Scripture and tradition, understood in light of the church's magisterium, needed to be reemphasized (Final Report, §II.B.a.1). We now have an opportunity to correct this neglect. As a dogmatic constitution of an ecumenical council, *Dei Verbum*'s influence is likely to endure a long, long time.

Subsequent Church Teachings on Scripture

Dei Verbum is surely the Catholic Church's most important teaching on revelation and Scripture in the twentieth century. As stated before, though, it neither resolved all issues relating to these themes nor is it the final word on such matters. The church has subsequently issued several key teachings that have promoted the Catholic appreciation of the Bible as the word of God. We might well consider them further fruits of the constitution.

One of the great strengths of the Catholic tradition is its long history of issuing formal, magisterial teachings on Sacred Scripture that give precise guidance to Catholic life. The Catholic Church is the only church to have such an official organ—the magisterium—to do so. So not only did *Dei Verbum* emerge from a long line of prior Catholic teaching on Scripture and revelation, but subsequently the church has continued to reflect deeply on the profound truths found in *Dei Verbum*. The following chart lists the most important of these subsequent documents. A short narrative comment will follow.

Church Documents on Scripture after *Dei Verbum*

Document	Year	Author	Content
Scripture and Christology	1984	Pontifical Biblical Commission	Published in two languages, Latin as the "official" text and French as the "working" text, there has been no official English translation issued (Italian and Hungarian translations are available!); published to help "pastors" deal with disputed issues on Jesus as the Messiah, based upon the Bible's teaching; the two versions sometimes differ significantly, making the document less user-friendly than is desirable
The Interpretation of the Bible in the Church	1993	Pontifical Biblical Commission	Issued on fiftieth anniversary of *Divino Afflante Spiritu* and one hundredth anniversary of *Providentissimus Deus*; instruction that analyzes all current methods of scientific biblical studies and

			notes strengths and weaknesses in them; rejects a fundamentalist approach for Catholics
Catechism of the Catholic Church (2nd ed.) 101–41	1997	Saint John Paul II	Essential and convenient summary of current church teaching on the Bible and how Catholics should interpret Scripture; given the nature of a catechism, the section on Scripture is short and concise
The Jewish People and Their Sacred Scriptures in the Christian Bible	2002	Pontifical Biblical Commission	Important statement about the Jewish people in the Bible; affirms the ongoing validity of the covenant between God and the Jewish people and recognizes the value of the Old Testament
The Bible and Morality: Biblical Roots of Christian Conduct	2008	Pontifical Biblical Commission	An analysis of the biblical foundations of Christian morality
Verbum Domini The Word of the Lord	2010	Pope Benedict XVI	Most important church document on the word of God since *Dei Verbum*; lengthy, poetic apostolic exhortation after the 2008 ordinary synod of bishops on the word of God; emphasizes a balanced approach to biblical interpretation, combining study and prayer, as well as *lectio divina** and a recognition of the liturgical settings of the Bible; acknowledges historical

Table continued on page 66

Document	Year	Author	Content
			critical method as an essential first step needing to be followed up by "spiritual" or "theological" interpretation; stresses continuity with Leo XIII, Pius XII, and *Dei Verbum* itself, spanning more than a century of Catholic teaching
Evangelii Gaudium The Joy of the Gospel	2013	Pope Francis	Although this lengthy apostolic exhortation does not formally address the Sacred Scriptures, as a new pope's first major solo teaching—which grew out of the 2012 synod of bishops on the new evangelization—it is notable for its frequent invocation of biblical images and themes and for its informal style; it underlines the crucial role of authentic preaching of the word of God and the simple truth of the gospel message; it exhorts all the faithful to join in the joy of proclaiming the good news of Jesus Christ

Pontifical Biblical Commission Documents

Despite the change in the status of the Pontifical Biblical Commission since 1971, when it no longer was considered an official "teaching" organ of the church, the Commission continues to perform an important service as a consultative body of experts for the Congregation of the Doctrine of the Faith. Indeed, the authority of the Commission's teachings is not really in question, since they are always issued by the Congregation with the approval of the pope. Thus, while they do not hold the level of authority of *Dei Verbum* itself or of papal apostolic exhortations, the teachings are part of Catholic tradition. As such, Catholics are invited to read and appreciate these teachings for their own enrichment.

The Commission has issued four documents since *Dei Verbum* that continue to expand Catholic understanding of the Scriptures. Of the four listed on the chart above, it's likely the instruction Interpretation of the Bible in the Church is the most significant. It is a comprehensive statement on Catholic approaches to the Bible. It analyzes in some detail most of the modern methods of biblical interpretation, noting the strengths and weaknesses of each method. Significantly, it says that no one method constitutes *the* Catholic approach to Scripture. It also highlights the historical critical method as "indispensable" but also insists on the need to go beyond it to other means of interpretation, including a judicious application of precritical approaches such as the fathers of the church. The document even notes the positive contribution to biblical scholarship made by some feminist interpreters or those coming from a liberation theology perspective or other modern approaches.

The other three documents—on Christology,[†] the Jewish Scriptures, and morality, respectively—address specific concerns from the viewpoint of Catholic tradition, biblical perspectives, and modern understanding. All three are significant in their own way, though the one on Christology is less useful since it is not available in an official English translation and is a bit more technical in nature. (An unofficial English translation by Joseph A. Fitzmyer, SJ, can be found at the Boston College website.[*]) The document on the Jewish Scriptures underlines the permanent value of the Old Testament, something already taught in *Dei Verbum* (14) but here fleshed out in much greater detail and nuance. The document on morality underscores the biblical foundations of all moral teaching and provides a helpful exploration of many biblical passages that contain ethical instruction. In short, all these teachings are part of the living tradition of the church underscored by *Dei Verbum*. The Biblical Commission, which likely will issue a document soon on the complex issue of biblical

[†] https://www.bc.edu/dam/files/research_sites/cjl/texts/cjrelations/resources/documents/catholic/pbc_christology.htm.

inspiration, has made and continues to make important advances in a Catholic understanding of Scripture and revelation.

The Catechism

In 1992 the first edition of the new *Catechism of the Catholic Church* appeared, a favorite project of Saint John Paul II as part of the renewal of the church leading up to the third Christian millennium that began with the jubilee year 2000. (A second, slightly corrected edition appeared in 1997.) The 1985 extraordinary synod of bishops on the promotion of Vatican Council II had also called for such a catechism (Final Report, §II.B.a.4). It is truly an impressive compendium of Catholic teaching through the ages, albeit updated with more recent church teaching. Its relatively brief section on Scripture outlines in a schematic fashion the essentials of Catholic teaching, but it is obviously not a full-blown explanation. As a catechism, its function is to serve as a summary and an authoritative resource. Unfortunately, at times the Catechism tends to refer to the Scriptures by using them as prooftexts* rather than offering solid interpretations of the texts, but this is perhaps to be expected in such a resource.

Unlike prior church catechisms that provided easy and simple question-answer formats, the new Catechism has more the character of a sophisticated resource to consult, not something to sit and read through. Fortunately, various bishops' conferences around the world, including in the United States, have produced slimmed-down editions that make the Catechism much more user-friendly. These more accessible editions exist for children and youth as well as for adults. The Catechism remains an important handbook for all Catholics, and Pope Benedict XVI drew attention to it on its twentieth anniversary (2012) as a tool for the "new evangelization" and the "Year of Faith" (October 11, 2012–November 24, 2013).

Verbum Domini *(Sept. 30, 2010, Memorial of Saint Jerome)*

Of all the post–Vatican II teachings on Scripture, Benedict XVI's postsynodal apostolic exhortation *Verbum Domini* is the most comprehensive and important. It grew out of the fifty-five propositions given to the pope from the twelfth ordinary synod of bishops in 2008 on the word of God. Interestingly, the Holy Father placed his teaching in the more than one-hundred-year-old tradition of scriptural teachings extending from Leo XIII, through Pius XII, to *Dei Verbum* itself. *Dei Verbum*, in fact, is cited some forty times in the text or footnotes, although sometimes the original force of the constitution is lost amidst the new context in *Verbum Domini*. Nonetheless, this is an indicator of the influence *Dei Verbum* has exercised on this papal document. The pope also takes the topic in a variety of creative directions to emphasize the need to make the Scriptures come alive for the church in our day. The very title, *Verbum Domini* (The Word of the Lord), is a direct allusion to the liturgical act of proclaiming the Word and responding to it, as we do at each Mass.

To promote this pastoral goal, Benedict XVI encouraged families to use the Bible for prayer, and urged all Catholics to rediscover the practice of *lectio divina* and a greater appreciation of patristic and medieval traditions of interpretation. At the same time, he reinforced the Biblical Commission's earlier 1993 teaching on the historical critical method as the "indispensable" starting point for biblical interpretation. He also favorably quoted the Biblical Commission's warning against fundamentalism, the one approach considered inappropriate for Catholics, since it basically disregards the incarnational view of Scripture taught in *Dei Verbum* (12–13).

Evangelii Gaudium *(Nov. 24, 2013, Solemnity of Christ the King)*

Pope Francis's first apostolic exhortation, written in his own style and with his own emphases, is the official outcome of the 2012 synod of bishops on the new evangelization. The pope clearly explained that while he used many propositions from the synod, he desired to write a document that addressed the theme of evangelization in a broader way. The result is a lengthy (288 numbered paragraphs) but highly readable teaching that ranges widely on the theme of announcing the good news of Jesus Christ in contemporary times.

This document does not explicitly address revelation or the Bible, yet it may be properly considered a "fruit" of *Dei Verbum* and the Second Vatican Council for two reasons. First, it explicitly promotes *lectio divina* (152) and making full use of the Sacred Scriptures in the task of evangelization. Like Benedict XVI before him, Francis also promotes the personal encounter with Christ that is essential for effective evangelization. Thus his perspective aligns well with the personal emphasis of *Dei Verbum*. A second aspect stands out as well—namely, the frequent use of examples from the Bible as illustrations and explanations of why the modern task of evangelization lies in continuity with the ancient tradition of announcing the good news of salvation.

One striking section of *Evangelii Gaudium* is directed to those who formally preach the word of God, especially priests and bishops. It treats at length the role of the homily in Catholic liturgy (135–59). Pope Francis calls the homily "the touchstone for judging a pastor's closeness and ability to communicate to his people" (135). He underlines the importance of the preacher's personal familiarity with the Scriptures through study and prayer and, at the same time, knowing one's flock (the congregation). Thus he attempts to bring people concretely in touch with Scripture and vice versa. Essentially, the section on the homily may be seen as an explicit explanation of his own method of preaching. From the beginning of his papacy, Francis has shown his ability to preach from the Bible simply and from the heart, always invoking biblical imagery and striving to give people concrete biblical examples for reflection. He also warns against making homilies too academic and too boring. In other words, one sees in this document a pastor who expresses himself frankly and underscores the role the Scriptures have played in his own ministry. This was also an express pastoral desire of the council. From this perspective, then, *Evangelii Gaudium* continues to place the Scriptures front and center in the church's call for renewal and for a "new evangelization."

A final note on these postconciliar documents is that, as with the documents of Vatican II itself, most of them are available on the internet, whether at the Vatican website (www.vatican.va) or elsewhere. Some have also appeared in eBook formats. So there is scarcely any excuse for interested parties not to utilize these resources.

The Debate over Methods of Biblical Interpretation

Since *Dei Verbum* appeared in 1965 there has been a flood of new methods for the study of Scripture. This has fostered a lively debate among scholars about the utility of the many methods currently employed for interpretation of Scripture. Of course, the dominant method throughout the twentieth century was the historical critical method, which essentially is a collection of diverse scientific methods for searching out the historical basis of Scripture. The roots of this method go back at least to the seventeenth century, but it took a long time for the results to catch up with Catholics.

No one can deny objectively that there have been many benefits from historical critical approaches to Scripture. Benedict XVI himself, though he saw limits to the method, acknowledged this, for instance, in his books on Jesus of Nazareth. But many criticisms have been leveled against historical criticism, some of them quite valid. For example, over-emphasizing historical questions has led to a downplaying or ignoring of spiritual teachings in the Scriptures. Also, some historical critics have made a practice of overly questioning the historical basis of the Bible with a hyper-skepticism that has left many faithful Christians wondering what they can believe. Another problem has been the exaggerated search for sources behind the Scriptures, or secular parallels from the ancient world, leading to a bewildering number of theories about "original" versions of biblical stories. Not only do they confuse many lay faithful but they also do not lead to any kind of spiritual enrichment.

This latter point is key. A big criticism of modern, scientific biblical studies has been its lack of encouragement of using the Bible for spiritual enrichment. Unfortunately, this is a valid criticism to a degree, but it does not take into account the enormous benefit that Catholics enjoyed from the scholarship of historical critics in the decades after the council. Not all historical critics of the Bible have fallen into the trap of ignoring spiritual messages. I think of late scholars like Raymond E. Brown, SS, Roland E. Murphy, OCarm, Eugene Maly, Barnabas Ahern, CP, Carroll Stuhlmueller, CP, Kathryn Sullivan, RSCJ, and others whose professional exegetical skills did not keep them from promoting a healthy appreciation of the spiritual messages of Scripture. Many of their publications were well received among the clergy and laity, and many Catholic biblical scholars became very popular speakers at conventions, religious education congresses, and biblical conferences. I also point to the great success of *The Jerome Biblical Commentary* (1968), edited by R. E. Brown, R. E. Murphy, and Joseph A. Fitzmyer, SJ, and its successor edited by the same trio, *The New Jerome Biblical Commentary* (1990), and the influence these have wielded for Catholics seeking enlightened interpretation of Scripture. (It is interesting to see that *Dei Verbum* 21, with its fatherly image of God reaching out to his "children," is cited on the dedication page of the NJBC, an indication of its pastoral intention.) Another example would be the highly successful commentaries of the *Collegeville Bible Commentary* (1992) and its successor, the *New Collegeville Bible Commentary* (2009–), published by Liturgical Press, with the former collected into a useful one-volume commentary. If space were available, other examples could be cited. Moreover, highly successful summer Scripture institutes have taken place that have helped shape Catholic study and preaching of Scripture (e.g., Georgetown University, Misericordia University, the University of Saint Mary of the Lake [Mundelein Seminary], and the Oratory Center for Spirituality in Rock Hill, SC). In fact, such Bible institutes continue to occur with regularity. Little Rock Scripture Study also offers one each year. All this is to say, one should not denigrate the achievements of those who have practiced the historical critical method with care and have attempted to communicate their research to a larger public.

Although the call for going beyond the historical critical method is valid, this has sometimes led to an overreaction. Some scholars have called for a return to precritical exegesis, like that of the patristic and medieval eras, when readers of the Bible did not have benefit of later linguistic, archaeological, and cultural insights. Today some older precritical commentaries are being made available in good translations. While this is a good development overall, one must be cautious about using such resources, because sometimes patristic and medieval interpreters were carried away with fanciful interpretations that had little relation to the biblical texts involved. One advantage of beginning with the historical critical method is that it roots us in the text itself. One cannot ignore the literal meaning of the text. The words must be understood literally before one can proceed to other levels of interpretation.

Although one cannot predict where these discussions will go, *Dei Verbum* and subsequent church teachings have indicated that Catholics should use all available means to help explore the depths of the Scriptures. Historical critical method has its limitations, but it is an essential starting point that cannot be wished away. One cannot legitimately turn back the clock to some ideal century and expect to be faithful in biblical interpretation. God's word, as *Dei Verbum* insists, is a living reality; it contains messages old and new that apply to God's people in every age. If there is a bit of a tug of war going on about method, I believe calm voices will win the day and finally help maintain a balance in Catholic Scripture study.

Implications for the New Evangelization: Prooftexting, Apologetics, and Proper Use of the Bible

With the concept of the new evangelization for the transmission of the faith taking hold in the wake of the synod on this theme in October 2012, the question of how Catholics can and should use the Bible has again risen to the fore. The new evangelization is an ambitious and visionary project to give renewed energy to the church's perpetual mission to proclaim the Gospel of Jesus Christ. However, it is not only outwardly directed to the "missions" or to areas of the world that have never encountered Christ. It is also inwardly directed to members of the church, especially those whose practice of the faith, for whatever reason, has diminished or ceased. For this reason, Saint John Paul II and Benedict XVI sometimes used the expression re-evangelization, though the preferred term is "new evangelization." It is a chance to hear the word of God anew and to get reenergized by it to carry it forth to others.

With this bold enterprise comes a temptation. Some Catholics have seen the call for the new evangelization as an opportunity to employ with new force the age-old method of apologetics. Apologetics is essentially a defense or explanation of the faith. In some modern circles, it has become a means to justify every aspect of Catholic faith by reference to Scripture. While defending the faith is certainly a valid tradition, which in some circumstances like outright persecution requires dramatic action, it also has some limitations. The most important one is that it sets one in opposition to those who do not share the faith. It immediately puts one on the defensive and in an argumentative stance. Moreover, attempting to justify every Catholic teaching, liturgical practice, or minor tradition with Scripture leads to prooftexting, that is, using passages of Scripture taken out of context to justify or prove the validity of one's belief or practice.

This option may be used appropriately in some circumstances, but it also goes against the spirit of the Second Vatican Council, and *Dei Verbum* in particular, which set a nonapologetic, nonconfrontational tone with regard to other denominations and even other religions. This does not mean that Catholics should not be proud of our faith or be afraid to defend it in the face of true persecution or ridicule. On the contrary, we have an obligation to defend the faith, but in ways that are consistent with the Gospel message and the example of Jesus himself. As the temptation stories in Matthew and Luke show, even the devil can quote Scripture (Matt 4:1-11; Luke 4:1-13). Throwing Scriptures back and forth at one another will achieve nothing (unless you are Jesus!).

Often, for any passage of Scripture one can find to defend a particular position, the opposite can be found somewhere in Scripture. One example is the teaching about plowshares and pruning hooks in the prophets. In one tradition, the one we quote to promote peace, God's word to the prophet is:

> He shall judge between the nations,
>   and set terms for many peoples.
> They shall beat their swords into plowshares
>   and their spears into pruning hooks;
> One nation shall not raise the sword against another,
>   nor shall they train for war again. (Isa 2:4; also Mic 4:3)

In another context found in the prophet Joel, we read the opposite as an exhortation:

> Announce this to the nations:
>   Proclaim a holy war!
>   Alert the warriors!
> Let all the soldiers
>   report and march!
> Beat your plowshares into swords,
>   and your pruning knives into spears;
>   let the weakling boast, "I am a warrior!" (Joel 4:9-10)

What is going on here? Did God change his mind? Which passage has the greater authority, since both are in the Bible?

The reason for this seeming contradiction is rather simple. Isaiah and Micah are prophets from the eighth century BC, and God's word to them addresses their particular context, their time in history, and their circumstances. In the face of threats to Israel's security by Assyria, the prophets advise peace and not war. Joel, on the other hand, is hard to date, though the book is certainly postexilic, thus considerably later, perhaps mid- to late-sixth century BC. It was a time of rebuilding and strengthening those who survived the exile, so God provided them words of encouragement and strength in the face of serious obstacles. They are called to fight for their survival. God's word came to these people in their proper context. Over time, contexts and circumstances changed, and God's word subsequently addresses these new situations in appropriate ways. Taken out of context, the words seem absolutely contradictory, which they are not. Both prophetic oracles have valid messages, but which is more appropriate for our day depends on how we understand this word of God to apply to us in our context. This example illustrates why it is so crucial to understand biblical passages in their context in the Bible. When people take the words out of context, misunderstanding almost certainly follows.

Perhaps another example is instructive. For centuries, Christian churches defended the practice of slavery because it was found in the Bible.

In fact, it is rather prevalent in the Bible, and even the New Testament does not have any condemnation of it. Yet, as explained by the Pontifical Biblical Commission's 2008 document on the biblical roots of morality (par. 110), only over time did the church's moral teaching about slavery change as gradual insight into the moral teaching of the Bible matured (see also *Verbum Domini* [VD] 42). Nowadays we recognize we cannot use the Bible to justify slavery. Responsible interpretation of the Bible, then, involves nuance and growth in understanding. One cannot simply cite Scripture literally without delving deeper into the larger questions of context, history, and the evolution of biblical interpretation over time.

So we should rejoice in the opportunity the new evangelization offers to use Scripture responsibly to bring others to Christ or to reignite the lukewarm faith of fellow believers, but we must avoid the pitfall of becoming pushy, confrontational, overly defensive, or fundamentalist.

Tasks for the Future

Pope Benedict XVI's encyclical *Verbum Domini* pointed out some areas where more work needs to be done by professional exegetes and theologians to help the church wrestle with some of the tough issues of biblical interpretation that were not resolved at Vatican II. Unsurprisingly, the nature of inspiration and the inerrant quality of Sacred Scripture constitute one area (VD 19). As mentioned already, this is a task the pope invited the Pontifical Biblical Commission to explore. Two more, of course, are refining our understanding of Scripture, tradition, and the magisterium and how they interrelate, and the "material sufficiency of scripture" (VD 17–18). These are rather technical issues, and I suspect it will take some time to develop them.

But the pope pointed to other areas where he saw the need for further work. These include the need for a directory on homiletics (VD 60) to help ordained ministers of the Word, who are charged with preaching the Gospel, better apprehend the Word they must preach and communicate it more effectively. He also called for more dialogue between pastors, theologians, and exegetes (VD 45) because the real value of the word of God is found when it is effective in the pastoral arena. This is where the word of God most urgently needs to be proclaimed and where its impact is felt most deeply.

Three more areas *Verbum Domini* points out for further work are continuing to make the Scriptures more widely available, especially by good translations into local languages (VD 115); increased appreciation and use of *lectio divina*, the prayerful reading of Scripture (VD 86–87); and establishing more centers for biblical formation (VD 75).

In other words, there is no lack of projects for the future. From *Dei Verbum* to *Evangelii Gaudium*, the Catholic approach to Scripture as God's holy, timeless, living Word has carried us a long distance. *Dei Verbum* prepared the path and set up the parameters for the discussion, but as the people of God move forward our encounters with the God of revelation in Scripture and tradition will require openness to further dialogue. God's hand of friendship never ceases to be outstretched to sinful humanity. The question is whether we are willing to grasp this loving hand in response.

Next Steps

Before concluding this book, I would like to propose a few possible next steps for interested readers. Perhaps the most important message that comes from *Dei Verbum* is the power of the word of God to reform the church and to nourish and strengthen us as God's people. In this constitution, Vatican II called for Catholics to make the word of God once more central to our lives. Although reading *about* Scripture and church teaching on Scripture is helpful, there is simply no substitute for reading Scriptures themselves. Thus my advice revolves around promoting familiarity with the Bible.

To this end, I recommend consideration of one or more of the following:

- Buy a recent Catholic study Bible and use it to help you explore the Scriptures. (You may also consider resources found in the recommended reading list below.)

- Read the Bible five or ten minutes a day for yourself. Hint: don't begin with Genesis and go to the end. You will soon bog down, right around Leviticus! Begin with smaller, more familiar books, like one of the gospels or a letter of Paul.

- Read and discuss short passages or stories from the Bible with your family.

- Learn an easy method of *lectio divina* and use it at least once a week for fifteen minutes of prayer with the Bible. Using a useful monthly resource like *Give Us This Day*, published by Liturgical

Press, can help you acquire good skills at *lectio divina* while using the liturgical cycle of readings for personal spiritual growth.

- Read the Sunday readings in advance so you can better understand them. (Most parishes publish the readings a week in advance; the United States Conference of Catholic Bishops website offers the readings for the entire liturgical year [www.usccb.org]. Another resource on the internet is Universalis [www.universalis.com], which has the daily readings and other resources available also in an unpaid format or an expanded edition through paid subscription. Another helpful monthly publication is *The Word Among Us* [www.wau.org].)

- Make the gospel of the liturgical year your main Scripture focus for the year. (Each liturgical year is dedicated to Matthew [Year A], Mark [Year B], Luke [Year C] in a repeating cycle. 2014 is the year of Matthew, 2015 is the year of Mark, 2016 is the year of Luke, and so on. John is used in the liturgical cycle every year, especially during the Lent and Easter seasons. You might consider concentrating on the gospel for the year in your study Bible, or even buying a new popular-level commentary on that gospel and use it throughout the year.)

- Consider joining or starting a parish Bible study with interested parishioners.

- Take time to attend a lecture on the Bible or a catechetical conference.

Conclusion

I hope that this brief overview of *Dei Verbum* in honor of its golden anniversary (2015) and in honor of the founding of Little Rock Scripture Study on its fortieth anniversary (2014) has helped you better understand recent Catholic teaching on Sacred Scripture from the Second Vatican Council and beyond. I conclude with the goal of the spread of God's word as expressed in *Dei Verbum*'s final paragraph (26):

> So may it come that, by the reading and study of the sacred books "the word of God may speed on and triumph" (2 Th 3:1) and the treasure of revelation entrusted to the church may more and more fill people's hearts.

Glossary

aggiornamento: an Italian word meaning "updating" or "reform"; used by Pope John XXIII to explain the main purpose of convoking an ecumenical council in order to make the truths of the faith more comprehensible in a modern context

anathema: from Greek *anathema* (accursed, separated from the fold), a word taken over in Latin and English to pronounce judgment on those opposed to the truth; historically this word was often used in official church teachings prior to Vatican II to defend the Catholic faith and condemn its perceived enemies

canon: from Greek *kanōn* (norm, rule), meaning the official list of inspired books of the Bible; the Catholic canon, fixed formally at the Council of Trent, consists of forty-six Old Testament and twenty-seven New Testament books

Christocentric, Christocentrism: making Christ the center or the focal point

Christology, christological: from Greek *christos* and *logos*, meaning the study of Jesus Christ (the Messiah)

Curia: the name given to the group of Roman congregations (offices or dicasteries) of the Holy See (Vatican) that help the pope govern the Catholic Church

deposit (of faith): the collection of sacred teachings or truths of the faith, entrusted to the apostles and their successors (see 1 Tim 6:20; 2 Tim 1:14)

Diaspora: the dispersion of the Jews throughout the ancient world after the destruction of Jerusalem and the temple in 587 BC; eventually this dispersion forced the translation of the Jewish Scriptures into Greek (the Septuagint) because the Jews began to lose their command of Hebrew in the context of life outside the Holy Land

dicastery (pl. dicasteries): from Greek *dikastērion* (court of law); technical word for a department of the Holy See, such as the various congregations, pontifical councils, tribunals, or other bodies of the Vatican's administrative structure

doctrine, doctrinal: from Latin *doctrina* (teaching); an official and authoritative teaching of the church; currently it is often used interchangeably with dogma, although a dogma is an infallible teaching

dogma, dogmatic: from Greek *dogma* (what is taught as an established tenet or object of belief); definitive and infallible church teachings of the highest authority pronouncing truths of the faith

ecclesiology, ecclesiological: from Greek *ekklēsia* and *logos*, meaning the study of the church

ecumenical: from Greek *oikoumenē* (inhabited world), referring to (a) worldwide gatherings of authorities such as a council or (b) interdenominational meetings or relations

encyclical: an authoritative letter issued by the pope on a given theme; this practice became more frequent among popes of the nineteenth and twentieth centuries

exegesis, exegete: from Greek *exēgeisthai* (to draw out or explain); technical word for the act of biblical interpretation by professional biblical scholars and commentators; contrasts with *eisegesis*, reading into the biblical text meanings that are not there

historical critical method: a generic title for a collection of modern methods using scientific and historical tools to explore the Bible, with an emphasis on seeking out the historical bases of Scripture

incarnation, incarnate, incarnational(ly): from Latin *in* and *caro* (flesh), literally "enfleshment"; the dogma of the eternal Word (Christ) becoming human or taking on human flesh (see John 1:14)

inerrancy: technical word for the literal verbal truth of the Bible; directly associated with "inspiration"; refers to the total lack of error—religious, scientific, historical—in the Bible; *Dei Verbum* avoids this term in favor of a more nuanced understanding of the truths in the Bible that are necessary for salvation being preserved by the Holy Spirit "without error"

inspiration: literally, "breathe into"; the concept that God mysteriously breathed his truth into Sacred Scripture by "inspiring" the human writers of the books of the Bible; many theories of inspiration have been proposed but not definitively accepted by the Catholic Church

intentional fallacy: a modern concept of the impossibility of knowing an author's intention from a written text, especially regarding the intentions of ancient, nonliving authors; thus the need for careful interpretation of texts

lectio divina: Latin for "holy or prayerful reading"; ancient practice of slow, prayerful meditation on Sacred Scripture; in the monastic practice this developed especially into the four main steps, *lectio* (reading), *oratio* (oral prayer), *meditatio* (meditation), and *contemplatio* (contemplation), a progressive set of stages to deepen one's understanding of the biblical message

Lectionary: a liturgical book of selected readings from the Scripture used at liturgy; after Vatican II, the Lectionary employed a three-year cycle for Sunday readings (Year A for Matthew, Year B for Mark, Year C for Luke, with John being used every year in special liturgical seasons like Lent and Easter) and a two-year cycle for daily readings

magisterium, magisterial: from Latin *magister* (teacher); the official, living teaching authority of the church

manual theology: the standard Roman approach to theology in the nineteenth and early twentieth centuries prior to Vatican II, wherein "manuals" or textbooks of collected teachings were used to educate priests and theologians; at Vatican II it became identified with a narrow and rigid approach to theology found in many Roman universities

material sufficiency (of Scripture): a technical theological concept that refers to the question of how much tradition adds to the teaching of revelation in Scripture or to what degree Scripture itself suffices for revelation

modernism: name given to the early twentieth-century theological crisis in the Catholic Church in the face of influences from science, secularism, industrialization, rationalism, and other modern influences that were deemed a threat to the faith; this perspective was condemned by Pope

Pius X in 1907; numerous theologians and biblical scholars were silenced for adopting the perspective of the "modern world"

nouvelle théologie: French for "new theology," a description of an early twentieth-century movement of French-speaking theologians in Europe who used ancient biblical, patristic, and medieval sources for a renewal of Catholic theology

peritus (**pl.** *periti*): Latin for "expert"; used of official theological advisors at Vatican Council II

pneumatology, pneumatological: from Greek *pneuma* and *logos*, referring to the study of the Holy Spirit

prooftext, prooftexting: using the Scriptures primarily to prove or defend a point, often taking the Scriptures out of context

rationalism: exaltation of human reason and scientific proofs based on demonstrable evidence

ressourcement: French, "going back to the sources"; a characteristic of proponents of the *nouvelle théologie* for the need to go back to biblical, patristic, and medieval Catholic traditions to promote revitalization in the church

revelation: from Latin *revelare* (to unveil or to make appear); making known miraculously what is hidden; the doctrine of (biblical) revelation can be viewed from a *propositional* angle, emphasizing various "propositions," teachings, or doctrines associated with God's self-communication with humanity, or from a *personalistic* angle, as in *Dei Verbum*, emphasizing the more personal, dynamic self-revelation of God to humanity

schema: from a Greek word meaning "outline" or "plan," this word was used for the draft documents prepared for debate at the Second Vatican Council; *De Fontibus Revelationis* was the first schema on revelation

Septuagint: from Greek, meaning "seventy"; Greek translation of the Hebrew Bible (Old Testament) done, according to ancient legend, by seventy translators working simultaneously to produce the same uniform text; often abbreviated with the Roman numeral LXX; became the basis of the Catholic canon of the Old Testament because it has a more complete canon than the Hebrew Bible

synod (of bishops): established by Pope Paul VI near the end of Vatican II (1965) as a consultative body for the pope, this assembly of bishop-delegates from around the world meets periodically in ordinary or extraordinary sessions to study given topics of current importance in the church; synods often produce a postsynodal document on the theme studied

theology, theological: from Greek *theos* and *logos,* meaning the study of God; can refer narrowly to (a) the specific view or analysis of God in biblical or church documents or, more broadly, to (b) a religious outlook

tradition: the sum and total of the scriptural, doctrinal, and liturgical teachings and practices of the church through the ages; distinct from "traditions" that are time-conditioned

Trinity, trinitarian: the dogma expressing the mystery of three persons in one God—Father, Son, and Holy Spirit

Vulgate: from Latin *vulgata,* "common"; designates Saint Jerome's Latin translation of the Bible from the original Hebrew and Greek to make the text more available to the common people of his day (ca. 340–420); today the "Neo-Vulgate," a modern version of the Vulgate edited by experts, serves as the primary Latin text of the Bible

Further Reading

English Translations of the Documents of Vatican II

Abbott, Walter M., gen. ed. *The Documents of Vatican II*. New York: America Press, 1966 and reprints. This is the earliest English translation of the conciliar documents, some of it done rather quickly. Some experts fault it for some misleading phrasing but it remains a useful resource. It is also available in a convenient and inexpensive eBook format.

Flannery, Austin, gen. ed. *Vatican Council II: The Conciliar and Post Conciliar Documents*. New rev. ed. Northport, NY: Costello Publishing, 1996. In addition to being a good translation, an advantage of this edition is the inclusion of many postconciliar documents.

Huebsch, Bill. *Vatican II in Plain English*. 3 vols. Notre Dame, IN: Ave Maria Press, 1997. A good rendering into everyday English the teachings of the council; serves well pastorally as a way to introduce people to the council but those desiring a more detailed understanding need to seek a more literal translation.

Tanner, Norman, ed. *Decrees of the Ecumenical Councils*. 2 vols. London: Continuum/ Washington, DC: Georgetown University Press, 1990. An expensive and technical version of all the ecumenical councils, but with original Latin or Greek texts on facing pages of the new translation, for those who can take advantage of them. On *Dei Verbum*, see vol. 2, pp. 971–81.

Selected Resources on Vatican II, *Dei Verbum*, and the Bible

Alberigo, Giuseppe. *A Brief History of Vatican II*. Maryknoll, NY: Orbis, 2006. A very readable and delightful account of the history of the council by the late undisputed leader of the "Bologna school" of interpretation of the council and who directed the technical and magisterial five-volume history of the council published in several languages.

Béchard, Dean P., ed. and trans. *The Scripture Documents: An Anthology of Official Catholic Teachings*. Collegeville, MN: Liturgical Press, 2002. An extensive collection of excerpts from Catholic teachings on the Bible, extending from councils to popes and documents of the Roman Curia.

Boadt, Lawrence, with Richard Clifford and Daniel J. Harrington. *Reading the Old Testament: An Introduction.* 2nd ed. New York/Mahwah, NJ: Paulist Press, 2012. A totally updated version of this classic basic introduction to the Old Testament by the late Father Boadt, filled with lots of background information.

Brown, Raymond E. *Responses to 101 Questions on the Bible.* New York/Mahwah, NJ: Paulist Press, 1990. This highly popular book began an entire series of appealing "101 Q&A" books on Scripture and other themes that helped disseminate widely sound information on the Bible and theology in a digestible question-and-answer format.

Faggioli, Massimo. *Vatican II: The Battle for Meaning.* New York/Mahwah, NJ: Paulist Press, 2012. A thoughtful, lucid, and informative discussion of the ongoing debates about how much Vatican II was in continuity or discontinuity with earlier councils and what is at stake in this debate.

Fitzmyer, Joseph A. *The Interpretation of Scripture: In Defense of the Historical-Critical Method.* New York/Mahwah, NJ: Paulist Press, 2008. A sophisticated series of essays on Catholic exegesis and why the historical critical method is indispensable. It includes an excellent chapter on the Pontifical Biblical Commission's document Instruction on the Historical Truth of the Gospels.

Hahnenberg, Edward P. *A Concise Guide to the Documents of Vatican II.* Cincinnati, OH: St. Anthony Messenger Press, 2007. A very helpful introduction to all sixteen documents of the council for the average reader with a view to encouraging people to read the texts themselves. Includes study questions.

Harrington, Daniel J. *Witnesses to the Word: New Testament Studies since Vatican II.* New York/Mahwah, NJ: Paulist Press, 2012. An excellent summary of progress in various areas of New Testament study since the council, done in a simple but comprehensive format.

———. *How Do Catholics Read the Bible?* Lanham, MD: Rowman & Littlefield Publishers, 2005. An informative simplified explanation of the Catholic approach to the Bible from the perspective of Vatican II.

Lysik, David A., ed. *The Bible Documents: A Parish Resource.* Chicago: Liturgy Training Publications, 2001. A fine collection of six prominent church teachings on the Bible, including *Dei Verbum*, with brief overviews and commentaries on them, though it lacks the most recent teaching, *Verbum Domini*, which only appeared in 2010.

O'Malley, John W. *What Happened at Vatican II.* Cambridge, MA: Belknap Press of Harvard University Press, 2008. An entertaining and sophisticated analysis of Vatican II that defends the notion that even the style of Vatican II indicated the theological shift that took place with this council. For more advanced readers.

O'Sullivan, Maureen. *101 Questions & Answers on Vatican II.* New York/Mahwah, NJ: Paulist Press, 2002. Following the popular question-answer format, this book gives many basic details about the council for the average reader; a good place for beginners.

Perkins, Pheme. *Reading the New Testament: An Introduction.* 3rd ed., rev. and updated. New York/Mahwah, NJ: Paulist Press, 2012. An updated version of this basic introduction to the New Testament with helpful background information as well as an overview of all the New Testament books.

Rush, Ormond. *Still Interpreting Vatican II: Some Hermeneutical Principles.* New York/Mahwah, NJ: Paulist Press, 2004. A readable and thorough presentation of issues and debates surrounding the ongoing interpretation of the council and its significance. For more advanced readers.

Senior, Donald, and John J. Collins, eds. *Catholic Study Bible.* 2nd ed. New York: Oxford University Press, 2011. A reedition of this Catholic study Bible using the New American Bible, Revised Edition (2010), which is the basis of the Catholic Lectionary. It has helpful introductory articles and the NABRE footnotes but not many other pastoral resources.

Upchurch, Catherine, Irene Nowell, and Ronald D. Witherup, eds. *Little Rock Catholic Study Bible.* Collegeville, MN: Liturgical Press, 2011. One of the most recent Catholic study Bibles, filled with practical charts, prayer starters, and information on archaeology and social justice, it utilizes the revised edition with notes of the New American Bible, Revised Edition (2010).

Witherup, Ronald D. *Scripture:* Dei Verbum. Rediscovering Vatican II. New York/Mahwah, NJ: Paulist Press, 2006. Part of an eight-book series on the sixteen documents of Vatican II, this is a user-friendly but more detailed summary of the origin, teaching, and impact of *Dei Verbum.* A "next step" book for those seeking more detailed information and bibliography on *Dei Verbum.*

———. *Saint Paul and the New Evangelization.* Collegeville, MN: Liturgical Press, 2013. An explanation of the 2012 synod on the new evangelization for the transmission of the faith, with a detailed proposal to use Saint Paul as a biblical model for the "new" evangelization today.

———. *Biblical Fundamentalism: What Every Catholic Should Know.* Collegeville, MN: Liturgical Press, 2001. A primer on the essentials of a Catholic approach to the Bible that avoids fundamentalism; also available from Liturgical Press in a Spanish edition.

———. *The Bible Companion: A Catholic Handbook for Beginners.* New York: Crossroad, 2009. An easy to read introduction to the whole Bible, with short summaries of the content of each book of both the Old and New Testaments, as well as essential introductory essays.